The Arsenic Lobster

A Hybrid Memoir

Peter Grandbois

Spuyten Duyvil

New York City

copyright © 2009 Peter Grandbois

ISBN 978-1-933132-72-3

Library of Congress Cataloging-in-Publication Data

Grandbois, Peter.
The arsenic lobster : a hybrid memoir / Peter Grandbois.
p. cm.
ISBN 978-1-933132-72-3
1. Grandbois, Peter. 2. Authors, American--21st century--Biography. I. Title.
PS3607.R3626Z46 2009
813'.6--dc22
[B]

2009019143

Intelligence is often the enemy of poetry, because it limits too much, and it elevates the poet to a sharp-edged throne where he forgets that ants could eat him or that a great arsenic lobster could fall suddenly on his head...

FEDERICO GARCÍA LORCA

We were at the beach
Everybody had matching towels
Somebody went under a dock
And there they saw a rock
It wasn't a rock
It was a rock lobster

THE B52's

FOR DAN

You are no artsy, fixer-upper. You are a cream colored house at the end of the cul-de-sac. A lone sapling aspen in your front yard (planted by the developer because they grow fast even though they can't survive long in lower elevations). You have no signage, no "water feature," no antennae, or "unnatural" colors. An edger hangs within easy reach in your garage.

Your neighborhood is called the "Dam West" because it is west of the "Dam East" and both are north of the dam that holds back the water from the Cherry Creek. Within the stone wall that surrounds your world run acres of green grass dotted by a cement turtle, a cement cheese—Oh, the hours you spent climbing that cheese! Backyards are intentionally small so that neighbors will spend time in the common lawns. You run along the paths from house to house, neighbors watching from the back porch like scientists monitoring rats in a maze.

Dave Cooks Sporting Goods is your playground. Woolworths, Walden Books, The Pet Shop, the Multiplex, Spencer's Gifts. It's 1973. Your father's layed off and your mother has to go back to work. You're nine and in charge of your seven-year-old brother and your six-year-old sister because the babysitter just let you watch TV. So, now you get paid for letting your brother and sister watch TV.

Family togetherness: *Donnie and Marie, Captain and Tennile, Shields and Yarnell, The Carol Burnett Show, Sonny and Cher, Columbo, All in the Family, Good Times, The Jeffersons, Alice, The Bob Newhart Show, The Flip Wilson Show, Happy Days, Laverne and Shirley, Love American Style, The Love Boat, Fantasy Island, M*A*S*H, Mary Tyler Moore, Maude, Mork and Mindy, The Odd Couple, 60 Minutes, The Waltons*...You'd like to say that you did your homework in the afternoon and so were free to watch TV all night., but that wouldn't be quite true: Afternoons were rerun time: *Hogan's Heroes, McHale's Navy, Gilligan's Island, I Dream of Jeannie, Bewitched, The Brady Bunch, The Partridge Family*, and (best of all) *Star Trek*. Somewhere in between or during these shows you managed to finish your homework, though you were always frustrated. Why couldn't you just watch Gilligan try to get the bowling ball off his hand?

Dinnertime. No TV. Exhausted from work, your mother showers while your father cooks. And every night for the nine years until you leave for college it's the same: hamburgers on the grill, Hamburger Pie, meat loaf, Porcupines (ground round patted into meatballs with rice), and on Fridays, chicken. Your mother has to have a clean plate, so when your father is not looking she scrapes her food onto your plate. You eat it and don't say anything.

Once a month you go out to McDonald's. Sometimes King's Family Host. Your favorite is King's Family Host because each booth has a phone you use to order. You loved the mystery of the voice on the other end of the line.

Born from the dust, conjured from the pages of Ray Bradbury, the Carnival arrives each summer. A pack of wild dogs, you and your friends ride your bikes down the dirt road that later becomes Peoria (complete with strip malls, a Chucky Cheese, a McDonalds, and a Dairy Queen). You watch them slowly set up the Ferris Wheel, the Merry-Go-Round, all the rides that spin and twirl. But you don't care about those because they make you motion sick. Every time you step on a ride that spins you throw up. The games are what interest you: skeet ball, fishing, pop the balloon, and get the ball in the milk can. That's the one with the shrunken heads. Skeletal white. Midnight black. Aged yellow. Some even a sort of puke green. All with long black hair. All with shriveled up lips, wrinkled faces. You spend your allowance trying to win, but you can't do it. (You don't need to think back on your life to know you've never won a single carnival game. Last summer in Reno, your seven-year-old daughter beat you at the horse race to win the stuffed penguin.) Your brother wins two shrunken heads, and shares one with you. You keep your head on the dresser beside your bed. At night, you swear it glows. You fall asleep staring into its cavernous eyes, and each night you dream of the South Pacific, of the Caribbean, of pirates and cannibals, and of darkness.

Mystery can't exist in the suburbs. Every Zenith 25" or Sony Trinitron banishes it to the outer dark beyond the hedgerows where the homeless dig through the garbage and the drunks masturbate at passersby. The roar of the lawnmower or leaf blower drowns everything.

You wrap your bikes in red, white and blue crepe paper. You wrap yourselves in American flags. Tie ribbons to your handlebars. Wear Uncle Sam hats. When you aren't riding your bikes in the parade, you're jumping up and down on the freshly mown green grass, waving your miniature flags as the fire trucks and police cars roar by, sounding their sirens. Grown men throw Jolly Ranchers, Fire Balls and Tootsie Rolls from open windows and the backs of trucks. Always there are veterans of war marching in uniform. You wave at them, and they wave back. Living G.I. Joes. (Never once an amputee rolling his wheelchair down the street). Swim races at eight sharp followed by pool games. Your favorite is the penny dive (hundreds—maybe thousands—of pennies dumped in the pool for the kids to fight over). Afternoon is filled with softball, a three-legged race, a water balloon and egg toss. In the evening, a German polka band plays in the park while your family spreads a magnificent summer feast upon your picnic blanket: potato salad, fried chicken, canned green beans, apple pie and watermelon. You eat and listen to music alongside your neighbors, sometimes even dance, but mostly you run around in front of the band and wait for dark when the fireworks begin. You love the fireworks, that's what Fourth of July is all about.

Wait. That's a lie. The bed race is everything to you. The event scheduled after the penny dive and before the softball game. Yes, the bed race.

You spent weeks preparing. You will not lose again to some middle aged, balding, hairy backed men dressed in tank tops, nylon shorts and expensive running shoes. You've taken your licks. The first time you and your friends showed up with a queen size bed still sitting on its metal frame with plastic wheels. It took you so long getting the bed out of the house you were almost late for the race. Then you saw your neighbors, supposedly fine upstanding businessmen, doctors, lawyers, and architects—each team carrying a twin mattress with a baby on top. No box spring, no frame, no little plastic wheels. And yes, the rules required a passenger sleeping in the bed. But a toddler! You at least had the decency to bribe your friend's five-year-old sister. You came in last that year, the friction with the pavement melting the plastic wheels half way through the course. In true cold war spirit, the next year you brought a twin mattress, again with your friend's sister on top. But it was not to be. Your neighbors came with sleeping bags and air mattresses. They no longer had a need to coordinate their efforts with other members of a team—one could do the job of two. Your team of four began to look antiquated—yesterday's business model.

This year it will all be different. Weeks of planning and preparation. Trips to the hardware store. Detailed measurements and specifications for what will surely be the Formula 500 of the bed race. And you won't be cheating like your neighbors; you'll use a full size bed encased in a wood frame, corners reinforced with extra nails. You'll sacrifice your best Kryptonite skateboard wheels (lime green). You'll mount the wheels on all four corners with Tracker Trucks (*Skateboard* magazine gave them their highest rating). You and a friend will push the bed from the front while your brother and another friend push from behind using carefully designed aerodynamic wood handles.

Race day. You arrive late. Let the other teams think they have a chance. You walk down Amherst Circle, heads held high (except your friend's sister who is seven now and embarrassed to be seen with you). It takes several candy bars to win her over this year. You imagined the neighbors would welcome your competitive spirit, praise your innovation, your drive to excel. But instead they file a protest with the referee saying you're cheating by using skateboard wheels. You point out that it's a bed race and you're the only team who actually has a real bed. An argument ensues. One of your neighbors even uses the "F-word." Your friend's sister starts to cry. She leaves the bed, saying she's not going to race. It's not worth it.

The deliberation is over. The judges take your side.

You beg her to race this one last time, then readjust the hockey helmet you made her wear (Safety first!), and she climbs back in the bed. The referee signals the start. Take your positions. The gun fires. Off to an early lead, you can almost hear the groans from the other teams as they begin to give up, shouting it's not fair. Only the clear blue horizon before you. But in the trial runs, you hadn't counted on the extra adrenaline of four crazed boys pushing with everything they had (Chaos Theory did not yet exist). The bed that behaved beautifully in practice now begins to swing hard to the right. Maybe the wheels are out of alignment. Maybe the front pushers are pushing harder than the back. You bark out orders to your team. Compensate by pushing hard left. But your nailed together wood frame is unable to cope with the stress at that speed. The back and forth motion proves to be too much, and the frame snaps, the mattress skidding along the pavement, your friend's sister tumbling toward the sidewalk.

You sit on the hot tar, dumbfounded, while each of your

monomaniacal neighbors races by. As you stare at the wrecked pieces of what was supposed to be the bed to beat all beds, their children, many of them your former friends, jeer at you from the sidelines. Wives—the same mothers who have often invited you into their homes for milk and cookies—now shout out encouragement to their husbands in the form of "Kick ass and take names!" And they do.

In fourth grade you carry your trombone to school every day until you develop a hernia. The doctor tells you: "Try something lighter." Your mother pays you $5 and gives you a John Denver songbook if you take up the guitar. In sixth grade, you play that guitar in a talent show and take second place, losing to a guy who mouthed along to the soundtrack of Barry Manilow's "I Write the Songs."

The name of your first band (you and your brother) is "Pumpernickel on Rye." Later, you're called "The Newspaper Boys," and "Peanut Butter and Jelly." Holidays you play concerts in the shopping malls.

You cannot escape your own inner suburbia.

You wait by the mailbox for the next TV Guide. Scan its pages for any movie with sword fighting in it, with a hint of the exotic: *The Road to Morocco, The Road to Zanzibar, The Sea Hawk.* The morning Errol Flynn's *Captain Blood* is on, you hold the thermometer next to a light bulb just like you've seen Peter do on *The Brady Bunch*. The thermometer burns your mouth. And though your mother isn't convinced, she lets you stay home. But you don't, do you? You're purchased as a slave by the beautiful Arabella Bishop only to escape and disappear into a life of piracy.

As soon as you hear the word fencing, see an image on a billboard, on TV or in a magazine (and corporations use fencing images all the time—it's so sexy), your senses overwhelm you. The smell of sour sweat mixed with leather, the clang of steel, the way the grip of the foil fits your hand like a small bird—you hold it delicately—the tunnel vision as the mask goes down. For that reason, it's difficult to sift through memory, to separate the decades of sensory experience and touch that first time you walked into the gym that held the university fencing club.

LESSON ONE: HENRI

Advance, advance. Retreat. His blade points at your chest. Beat quarte flank, disengage sixte, riposte with glide to high line. Advance. Beat sixte, one-two, parry four with pris de fer and advance lunge. Within a few minutes, your legs falter, your sword arm weakens.

"Faster, Peter."

Beat quarte direct. Advance. Beat disengage. Advance. Beat coupe. Advance. Beat sixte direct. Beat sixte disengage. Beat Coupe. Lunge. Lunge. Lunge. Lunge."

"Faster, Peter. Harder."

Beat octave direct. Advance. Beat coupe flank. Advance. Beat seven belly. Advance. Beat seven feint belly, coupe chest. Lunge. Lunge. Lunge. Lunge.

"What's the matter, Peter?" he asks. Always the same. "You are slowing down. You must be fast. Strong. Now show me *En-garde*. That's it. Hand back. Knees straight. Form is everything."

Engage blade quarte. Advance lunge. Engage quarte. Disengage. Advance lunge. Engage quarte. Coupe. Advance lunge. Lunge. Lunge. Lunge. Lunge. "One more, Peter. One more." Lunge. "One more, Peter."

"I can't."

"One more."

Lunge. Lunge. Lunge. Lunge. Lunge.

The day after you visit your seven-year-old sister in the hospital, see the left side of her body paralyzed from the stroke, you go to stay at a friend's house so that your parents can stay with her. A wounded robin sits in the shaded grass out back. You and your friend get straws and a bag of un-popped popcorn. You kneel on the ground a few feet from the bird and shoot corn kernels at it through your home-made blow guns. The bird shrieks back at you, but you keep firing.

You keep two shoeboxes for your future astronauts—one for the lizards you catch in the field and another for the grasshoppers. The next morning the lizards are gone, escaped somehow despite the fine furnishings in the shoebox provided by your sister's Barbie collection. You search the house for remains, afraid the dog may have eaten them. They probably met a better fate than the one you had in store for them in the payload compartment of your Estes Rocket. No matter. In place of lizards, there's always grasshoppers. They will be your next Neil Armstrong and Buzz Aldrin. And more often than not they will crash back to earth (the parachutes on the Estes Rockets rarely opened correctly), and you will wonder what they must have thought as they're shot three hundred feet straight up. Do they yearn to breach the atmosphere? Is that brief glimpse of beyond worth the free fall back?

The astronauts are the lucky ones. They escaped your death camps. You read in a library science book that you can freeze grasshoppers and then thaw them out—and they'll live! You test the theory. First fifteen minutes, then an hour, then a day. They can survive up to an hour. More than that it's a crap-shoot. Next you try the opposite, extreme heat. They never last more than a few seconds in the microwave. At least they die in the name of science.

Bow hunting carp in the Cherry Creek Reservoir. (Yes—bow hunting carp) You and three friends armed with bows prowl the swamp that feeds the reservoir. At the sight of a fin in the water, a splash, the slightest ripple across the surface, you let loose a slew of arrows. Floyd plays the scout. When the fish takes off through the shallows, he gets so excited he chases it. Arrows fly past his head, his torso, missing him by inches. You know this is not a good idea, but you say nothing. And then you get one. No one knows whose arrow hits the giant carp first, pinning it to the ground. But soon you're firing at will into it. It keeps breathing, tail lashing. You want to leave, but you don't. Not even when Vince smashes its head in with a big rock.

You don't feel any better as you extract the arrows and pile them into your rubber raft. The plan is to float back to the car across the reservoir, but you don't count on the rising winds, the thunder clouds darkening the water. Half way across, the raft sinks (too many holes from the arrows). Vince says he can swim it. You and Floyd tell him he's crazy, then swim to a nearby buoy, holding the bows above water all the way. The rain pours, and Vince is a dot in the distance. By the time the coast guard picks you up, you are sure Vince has drowned, penance for the carp. But on the way in, the coast guard spots him. He wouldn't have made it otherwise. Now Vince photographs strippers for a living.

What demon moves you to stick Black Cats under stink-bugs? You prop them up on the firecracker—forelegs on the ground, ass riding the Black Cat, struggling to escape, watching the slow burn. Sometimes at night you imagine you still have stinkbug guts in your hair. No matter how hard you try, you can't get it out. Even now. Even now.

Henri is a real French, fencing master. He even graduated with a degree in fencing from the University of Paris. A degree in fencing! You still can't believe it. You've never seen reflexes that fast, a hand that, without seeming to move, can defend and strike back before the opponent has time to react. He fenced for Lebanon in the 1984 Olympics but was told to forfeit when he drew the Israeli team. He was not even allowed to meet the Israeli on the strip. He teaches you the basics: how to keep distance so that you only need to move your hand an inch to defend your entire body; how to move as if your feet don't leave the floor; how to take the blade before you advance so that if your opponent deceives you, you have time to recover. But he can't give you his speed. You have to be born with that kind of speed. You're fast, but you'll never be that fast. And even if you were, where would you run?

As an undergraduate and in your first master's degree, you specialize in medieval literature and Old English. Even then you understood the need for anachronism, the need to devote yourself to something completely outside the carefully measured square footage of your suburban lot (7,543 sq ft.—lots were bigger in those days). You want to spend the rest of your life studying something that no one else understands, something that will blot out who you are, where you came from.

Fencing is also an anachronism. As George Carlin once joked in his sports routine: "Fencing's not a sport because you can't bet on it!" And so, you memorize *Beowulf,* and you take fencing lessons—thousands and thousands of fencing lessons.

And Henri is the older brother you never had. You spend hours at his house learning to wire the blades, to fix and maintain your equipment. He tells you there's no excuse for poorly maintained equipment, that a champion fencer goes on strip never having to worry if his equipment will function. A champion focuses all his concentration on the match. And you listen, and you learn. You soak in everything, from the way he holds himself, to the dirty French songs he sings, to the pride he demands of you—a pride you've never let surface before because each time you walk into the gym, hear the clang of steel, hold the foil in your hand, you feel the need to erase the person you once were, the person you still are. Coming from the suburbs, fencing is a trip to feudal Japan. And so you bow your head before your master, beg him to be swift. The cut is clean. Your head falls to the floor, stares back at you.

"One more time, Peter."
"I can't."
"No excuses."
"But I can't breathe, Henri."
"Lunge."
You lunge, but it is feeble, sloppy.
"Again."
"I can't."
"Again."
"Again."

A tunnel into the dark earth, even if it only goes a few feet in, is a gateway to another world. You tell yourself that when the paramedics and fire trucks come to dig out the nameless sixth grader who is trapped when his tunnel in the gulley beyond the school yard caves in. He nearly suffocates, and you wonder what his last minutes were like before he lost consciousness.

They fill in the tunnel and send announcements home warning about the dangers. But even in a suburb there are any number of gateways to the unknown.

The giant boa (you remember it as monstrous, but it really couldn't have been more than six feet long—could it?) must have escaped from a neighbor's terrarium. Orange with dark spots—it seems so exotic, was it really that color? A suburban Alice, you grab its tail as it goes down a hole in the dry dirt of the field behind your elementary. You tell your friend to get help. After that, the memory is fuzzy. You imagine the tug-o-war with the snake, the way you set your feet in the ground and lean back, digging in for the fight, then the horror as you slowly realize you're losing. The snake pulls you forward, inch by inch into its hole. You're on your stomach, holding on with both hands, anchoring your toes into the earth. You're sure you let go only once the snake pulled both your arms deep into its damp hole. It was then your mind played tricks on you. The remains of countless little boys lie scattered within.

The sewage line empties into the gully and runs beneath Peoria Street. Made of cement, it's just big enough to walk in hunched over (at least at age nine). Each time you pass by, you swear a voice calls out to you from within. You go alone. You take only a book of matches. Not much oxygen. The matches go out almost as soon as they're lit. But not before you catch a glimpse of shifting shadows along the walls. Your bare feet squish down through mud, jerking back at soft, slimy things—hairy things that make you think of rotting rats. You climb the ladder that leads to the manhole on Peoria and listen to the cars overhead. You put your mouth to the holes in the cover, take a deep breath of the outside atmosphere, but find you prefer the fetid air beneath the surface of your known world.

And then there's the spillway beneath the Cherry Creek Reservoir. You skateboard there at age eleven, twelve, thirteen—the best full pipe anywhere. Occasionally, you dare each other to walk the length of the giant pipe through the darkness beneath the dam. (An iron gate covers that pipe now.) You walk the distance alone, cars thrumming overhead, driving across the dam, driving over you. The rumbling belly of the whale. The air is so thick it hurts. With each step, it gets harder to breath. And then the giant, steel door before you. The last few steps are the worst, as if the weight of all that water and earth exerts a force pushing inside your head. *No one will know if you turn and run, if you tell them you touched the door.* For some reason you continue right up to the massive steel and reach out your hand. And when you touch the door, you're sure it's damp. Wet from water leaking in around the edges, through the pores.

You dig tunnels in the dirt and snow. You make forts under blankets. You create labyrinths with cushions from the living room couches. You lose yourself in the dark so you can feel the breath of the Minotaur on the other side.

You construct your most elaborate maze every Halloween in your friend Scott's basement. His dad is a doctor. He has a complete skeleton of a young woman—and it's real! So you spend weeks planning your haunted house, hang blankets from the exposed pipes in the basement ceiling. And at the center of your labyrinth, the skeleton rocks back and forth in an antique rocking chair, a butcher knife in her hand, fishing line connected to her jaw, her hands (operated by your brother). You volunteer to do the test run over and over. You wind your way in the darkness as ghouls jump from hidden doors. You turn the corner, knowing what waits there. The strobe light temporarily blinds you. The skeleton screams and raises the knife, blood dripping from the tip.

The lone, decrepit house stands in the middle of the field at the edge of your world. Why don't they tear it down? It's an eyesore, your neighbors say. Your parents tell you never to go near it. But you do. You and two friends (maybe your brother) enter the house one afternoon after school. The place wreaks of rotten fruit, of trash left out in the sun, a towel starched with years of body odor. You open the bathroom door and see the bloodstained sink. The rag with spots of red lying on the floor. You go to find your friends in the kitchen, but they've already run out the back door, screaming. What did they see that made them run so fast? What did they imagine they'd seen?

Five Points is not your normal hangout, but the fencing club has moved and you and Henri want a beer. The shot cracks the cold October night. You turn, wide-eyed, wondering at the sound, but Henri has already grabbed you, thrown you to the cement. "Don't move," he whispers as he pans the darkness, his hand gently but forcefully pushing against your back, keeping you to the ground. He grew up in Beirut during the civil war. He recalls as a child witnessing the slaughter of hundreds of Palestinians by the Christians in the street in front of his house. He doesn't tell you that story until many years later.

You take second place in your first tournament—a competition open only to beginners. Henri says you show promise, and by then anything he says is gospel. But you take sixteenth in the next tournament—an open, losing to a guy you could have beat. With every touch you score, he throws his mask, his foil. He storms up and down the strip. And you remember thinking, if he loses he'll never recover. But if I lose, so what? So you let him score. Oh, you make it look good—you move your feet, try to block his attacks just a fraction too late. Then after, with the most sincere look you can muster, you tell him "Nice fencing." But the truth is, the loss eats at you. And Henri never understands. He says you have to have pride in yourself, that it's embarrassing to lose like that. You think about it for weeks afterwards. Months later, you lose to a cadet at the Air Force Academy, a cadet you can clearly take. Henri turns from you in frustration. "I don't understand, Peter," he says. "Don't you have any pride?" But you can't make him understand. You drive the hour and a half home from Colorado Springs feeling like you have to shit the whole way, holding it, but when you arrive home it doesn't come.

You lose many, many tournaments. But at some point you realize your need to win. So, each and every morning you meditate. Hypnotize yourself (Yes, you are a child of self-help books!) *You're facing the tricky kid from Chicago who likes to duck, and you're down four to zero. Acknowledge the voice that says to give up. Then stab the fucker.* You commit countless murders each and every day. Brutally, you stab the corpse, slit its throat and drag it down the dark alley of your unconscious. And after a few years of daily assassinations, you walk onto the strip at the 1989 Rocky Mountain Sectional Championships in Tucson, Arizona and you take no prisoners.

After Tucson there's no looking back. You've tasted pride, and one sip can fill you for weeks after. You fly to Dallas, Los Angeles, Kansas City, Omaha, London (Ontario), Chicago, San Antonio, New

York. When you sleep on the jets, you dream fencing. You wake to the movements of your hand as it works through imaginary bouts: parry six, pris de fer, thrust to the flank. In Chicago, you lose in the first round of your first North American Cup to the Canadian National Champion. But you make him work, and that's what counts. In New York, you take out three of the four members of Yale's team. In Los Angeles you show them what training and attention to classical form can do as you hit with a tight parry riposte and a disengage thrust more times than is possible. You become addicted to the slow distillation of time, the drip, drip of seconds as you zone in on your opponent's chest. Then the great surge as, without thought, your body reacts to your adversary's thrust, your body, not your brain, thinking two steps ahead and knowing that thrust is really a feint that will be followed by a disengage to the six line because a few moves back he tested that very scenario. Your body knows and gives him the oversized parry four he wants, shows him the target just below the shoulder. He commits. Take the blade in six and ram it home, touché!

Warning: In case you haven't noticed, there is no story here. You're no Eisenheim, and you doubt that even his necromantic skills would be able to turn this fight into an ordered timeline, progressing forward with due emphasis on how said narrator (in this case "you") got into this mess. This is war, pure and simple. Anything else is falsification. Inauthentic. Let's leave the narrative arcs and epiphanies to those who need them. You know better, don't you?

LESSON TWO: GARY

Put down your foil. Close your eyes. You're in a bubble that extends six feet out from your center. See that bubble around you. Feel it. You're safe within it. But as soon as your bubble touches your opponent's bubble you'd better be attacking or you're dead. Within the bubble, you're only preparing to attack. Playing mental chess. Setting up your defense three moves in advance. Everything you do before you close the distance is preparation—it sets up your final thrust. *But what if my opponent attacks outside of my bubble?* Ignore it. *What if at the point of contact he attacks before I do?* Then you're dead. Never forget. Your opponent is also manipulating the distance, doing everything he can to get inside your bubble. *So how do I make sure to attack first?* Therein lies the secret of fencing. Let him think he's manipulating the distance better than you. Give him the distance he wants, then take it away. Attack before he realizes what happened. *Isn't that risky? Don't I chance letting him get too close?* You can't win without risk. Be thankful it's only a game. Now put on your mask and take up your blade, but don't use it. Show me how you manipulate the distance with your feet alone. Your hand stays still. *But why do I need my mask if I'm not attacking?* The strip appears different from within the mask. Your opponent appears different. Though it's only a lesson, it should feel as close to real life as possible.

Can you court risk in the suburbs? Let us count the ways:

Take your father's bow, his practice arrows (not the razor sharp deer hunting arrows but the pointed metal ones that could still pierce a man from a hundred yards). Gather your friends around and point the bow with arrow loaded toward the heavens. Let fly. Now see which one of you can catch it by the shaft on the way down. You're good. Very good. You wait, feet firmly planted, arm outstretched before you. Watch the black dot against the blue as it grows bigger, bigger. Don't flinch. Don't let the fear take you.

Floating down the highline canal. You pump up a queen air mattress and your inflatable raft (you know, the one with the holes you already punctured in it from your adventure on the reservoir, the one you thought you'd repaired). You pack a lunch of peanut butter and jelly, donuts, chips, hot tamales—the usual fare. You take two cars, drop one several miles down the canal so you'll have a way to get back. You knew the canal water was filthy. In fact, you heard they tested it the month before for Typhoid. But now you see the six-pack plastic rings and Doritos bags, the beer cans and McDonald's Styrofoam containers floating along the surface. You make most of the trip down the canal halfway underwater because the raft has already started to sink. Of course, the food is soaked. You eat it anyway. You worry only slightly about the rats diving in and out of the canal along the banks. Only occasionally do you imagine them chewing on your toes.

Four hours later. The police search the brush above the river, calling for you to come out. You hug tight to the bank until the cops leave, only then climbing the steep ravine barefoot through cockleburs. You abandoned your shoes in the raft when the cops appeared. And so you spend the rest of the afternoon walking through fields, pulling stickers from your bare feet, looking for your car. And you remember the flash of orange, the surge of red as the sun set over the golden field. You remember your dry, cottony mouth. Remember drinking from the water bottle even though you feared it might have been polluted. You remember, the dozens of stinging pin pricks from the cockleburs stuck to your feet, ankles and calves. You remember all this because you never felt more alive.

Fields are dangerous places for boys, and your suburb is an island in a sea of fields. You're sixteen, or maybe it's your oldest friend who is sixteen. You remember him, see his face clearly. The goofy smile. The smile that strikes you now as tired, as if by sixteen he'd already lived too much. Maybe that's why in all those years you never once went to his house to play. No matter. Now you're in the field, and all bets are off. *Out beyond ideas of rightdoing and wrongdoing, there is a field. I'll take you there.* (Even Rumi knew.) Everyone is equal in the fields, but some are more equal than others. (Orwell also had it right. Golding, too—he knew what happened to boys when left alone in fields.) You take turns hanging on to the top of your friend's green '73 Ford Pinto while he drives through the dirt and rocks, turning and spinning in an attempt to throw you off. And all the while he's smiling.

In yet another field, across Peoria and Yale, you take the same friend's car over jumps. Rev the engine down the runway, hit the dirt ramp at forty, the feeling of weightlessness as you float near the roof of the car, then the pain as you land in the seat first, the boom box landing on your head. When you tire of that, you take turns sitting in a saucer sled tied to the back of the car as your friend drives—twenty, thirty, forty miles per hour, the glint in his eyes shining brighter with each hash mark on the speedometer. You're so scared you can't take your hand from the rope to give him the thumbs down signal to slow—not that he'd slow down anyway. The ride ends when you hit a rock or a bump then shoot through the air, bouncing over rocks and yucca plants.

And nothing beats "Skatewars" for blood. Your own *Rollerball*. The hill behind the Dodge dealership on Hampden Avenue is perfect because no cars ever use it. The goal: to crash into each other at full speed and see who survives. Some of you stand up, others ride on your knees, others on your stomachs, making a battering ram with your head and hands. Every scar is a badge. You win the arms race with the six-foot long speed board you and your brother designed, built from a plank of wood two inches thick and eight wide. Soon, Skatewars becomes obsolete. No one can stand up to the "Haulboard." Now it's all about speed. Someone rides a bike with a speedometer alongside the board while you ride it on your stomach, arms extended for maximum aerodynamics. Ten miles per hour, twenty, twenty-five, the bicyclist can't go faster than that so you don't know your actual top speed—thirty, thirty-five, maybe even forty! At some point, the board begins to vibrate, then wobble. If you panic you fall, rolling and scraping along the pavement. In the days before safety, you're smart enough to wear hockey helmets, but knees, bellies and elbows don't fare so well. Conquering warriors, you march home.

If you could but survive "Skatewars," if you could master the speed of the "Haulboard," the suburbs had nothing on you.

What if my opponent is faster than me, Gary? Speed doesn't matter. What matters is the set up. What matters is who is smarter.

But if I can get in and out quickly? It's all in the preparation. If you prepare correctly, you can hit with a single thrust moving with the speed of a snail.

Ruby Hill. The highest sledding hill in Denver. Your winter paradise. Not content to sled where everyone else does, you sit your toboggan atop the iciest, steepest part of the hill unaware of the Olympic style ski jump at the bottom. Three of you sit in the sled while one (the older kid with the car and the smile) stays back to push. He digs in. Then, shoves off, pushing you in true Olympic bobsled fashion. At the last, he sacrifices himself with a final shove, falling on the ice to give you that extra something. When you soar a few feet in the air off the first small bump, you know you're going faster than anyone has ever gone in a recreational sled before, faster than anyone has a right to go without paying the price. Suddenly, you're worried.

You look ahead to see a fence at the bottom of the hill on the left. You could hit it. But your brother, also startled by that first jump, looks ahead in terror only to note a row of trees on the right. So, you lean right, and he leans left. As a consequence, you continue straight ahead and hit the ski jump neither of you has seen.

If you could find one of the children looking on from that day, a nine-year-old boy who, perhaps, now works for an energy firm in downtown Denver, one with a young child himself, maybe another on the way, what would he say? Would he talk of how three kids flew higher than the trees? Would he mention the hushed silence that fell over the onlookers at the top of the hill? Would he remember how the lone pusher, thrilled at the sight of his compatriots soaring through the air, jumped up and down like Smeagol having at last bitten the One Ring from Frodo's finger? Or would he remember only his own nearly-frost-bitten toes? Or the fact that his father had worked yet another Saturday and dropped him off on Ruby Hill to sled with his only friend? Would he remember anything at all, really? Was he even paying attention when three kids graced the heavens, flying nearly forty-six feet?

And what about you? Do you remember the wind whipping through your ears? The stifled screams as you take flight (from you or the crowd you're not sure)? And then the silence: the way the air stops conducting sound? Do you remember thinking this is what it's like to fly?

It is enough that you remember the sharp hush of the world, and it is beautiful. But beauty overwhelms, and then you black out.

Wrap the tape around your pointer finger, then once, twice, three times around your wrist. Test it to make sure it holds tight, supports the pressure on your finger when you take up the foil. Test it on Henri's chest. Extend. Aim.

Lunge. The tension in the blade metastasizes, piercing your pointer finger to your elbow.

"Why are you taking so many lessons, Peter?" Henri asks. You've finally told him about the lessons two nights a week with Gary.

Lessons in addition to the two he gives you. "They can only take you so far," he continues. "At some point you have to fight."

You tell him you got in the game late. "There is so much to learn."

"You've drilled enough," he says. "Too much." He pulls off another strip of tape, rips it in two with his teeth. Takes your hand in his and pulls the strip tight about your finger. "Do your learning on the piste."

"Firecracker Wars." Every holiday has its rituals—all of them dangerous. Once you hit the teenage years, every Fourth after the sanctioned fireworks, you gather with your friends in the field, each armed with a backpack full of Black Cats, Pop Bottle Rockets, Jumping Jacks (Don't you just love the way they whiz about so unpredictably?), and, of course, a few Roman Candles. You wear goggles, jean jackets, and gardening gloves to protect yourself from the sparks (always safety conscious). You divide into teams—a mere formality because soon it will be each man for himself.

Your brother closes the distance, blasts a blue fireball past your ear, laughing maniacally. Later, when you've called a truce, you pull out one last Roman Candle. Shoot the fireball into your friend's backpack. You note the terror on his face as he struggles to rip it off. You observe his macabre dance in the flickering light as Black Cats boom, Jumping Jacks whiz, and bottle rockets hiss, firing in every direction. And even as you worry about him catching fire, you laugh—you can't stop yourself.

"Once inside the bubble," Gary reminds you. "If you hesitate for a second, you are dead."

"So speed matters after all."

"Yes," Gary says, taking off his mask, nodding his head as if you've finally got it. "But not physical speed." He pauses. He wants to be sure you are ready for his last gift. "The speed at which you are willing to kill or be killed."

It's the finals of the Kansas City Open, and you feel like shit. You drove in late last night, stayed in a flea-bag motel on the edge of town only to lie awake as your neighbor pounded on his girlfriend's door all night begging her to give him a second chance. You've fenced horribly through the early rounds, barely making it into the finals, and now you're losing eight to three in a fifteen-touch direct elimination bout. You give your opponent the distance he wants. Draw him in. But you're sluggish. Your movements are too big, and he counter-attacks into your preparation. His point hits your hipbone, hard. The blade snaps, the shaft piercing your thigh. At first, you think nothing has happened, but then you look down and see the circle of blood slowly spreading across your knickers. Your friends carry you to the side of the strip. They tear your pants off and wrap a shirt around the wound. Still the blood pumps out. Someone mentions calling an ambulance, but you tell them you'll be all right. You know you will. The referee says you have twenty minutes to recover or forfeit the bout. Why don't you quit? your friend, Andre asks. You don't answer. Instead, you put your pants back on and walk back to the strip. Your opponent's face pales. Your entire thigh is stained red. A crowd gathers. The referee calls you to *En-garde. Allez!* When you attempt to move, you go woozy all over. Better to stay in one place.

Keep it simple. But it doesn't matter. Your opponent has forgotten how to fence, his eyes fixed only on your thigh. His attacks are feeble, easy to parry. And with each thrust you drive into his chest, your world closes about you. A vortex. Another snake hole. Only you and your opponent exist. Circle four parry, riposte. Octave coupe to the back. You don't want to climb out. Everything exists for you here. But when you do, Henri is proud.

A white, '69 Chrysler Plymouth with six-foot Water Buffalo horns mounted on the front, "Le Moo" written in thick black marker across a red banner hanging from the center. A fake rubber hand stuck out the back trunk. Your car is legendary, and you practically live in that legend with the black vinyl seats, taking your friends to and from school, play practice, band practice, gigs. But best of all are the nights you, your brother and your friends cruise the back roads. Turn off your lights and drive as fast as you can. *Use the force!* Count how many seconds you can do it before palms sweat and your heart skips a beat. Next, cruising Colorado Boulevard. You're straight out of the fifties except your goal isn't to pick up girls. It's to act as ridiculous as possible. You're overjoyed by the befuddled looks you get from graying men in BMW's as you shadow them dressed as Dracula. You're practically orgasmic when a pickup truck full of jocks gives you the finger for driving near their car dressed as the sweet transvestite from Transsssssexual Transylvania. Get them to chase you and ram the pedal home. Can they use the force too? Faster and faster. You've got to make the jump to light speed! Yes, a night devoted to "shock and awe" can sustain you at least until after breakfast.

When you're not acting out, you're acting. Always trying on another face. As a high school freshman, you try out for the spring musical—*Bye Bye Birdie*—You stand alone on stage in front of the drama director and the music teacher, and you drop to your knees. "Massa," you say. "Lawdy, Massa, don't let them take me down river!" (At least that's the way you remember the line.) The only thing you can't figure out is who entered your body and turned you into a thespian. You're the shy kid. And yet you sing "I Got Plenty 'O Nothing" and garner the lead. It's not your only role. You sing The Beatles "I'm a Loser," and get the lead in another musical, *The Fantastiks*. (The director jokes about your tendency to sing self-deprecating songs to win roles.) You play a drifter in *The Rimers of Eldritch,* Demetrius in *A Midsummer Night's Dream,* Motel in *Fiddler on the Roof,* one of the disciples in *Godspell,* a chorus member in *Pippin*. In other productions you're assistant director and stage manager. You even direct, produce (with a budget of $36) and star in two different one-act plays (one by Woody Allen, the other by your friend Mike). You and Mike make films—most notably a Star Trek parody in which you play Kirk. Yes, you're Woody Allen, Mel Gibson, Warren Beatty, and Clint Eastwood all rolled into one. At the same time you compete in football and track, sing in honors choir before school, form a barbershop quartet that performs evenings around town, and, of course, play in your own rock band. It exhausts you even now to think about it. You wake at six and go to bed at midnight, every moment filled with activity. Stay off the streets. What does it matter if in the suburbs the worst that can happen on the streets is that you might see your neighbor naked in the window?

So, you never stop. Never. And yet look at you standing there in the photo, surrounded by thespians in your high school drama club all in motion, acting crazy. There you are, the still point in the center, the sad face of a clown, set at a distance from all the activity. Inside, your pulse pounds, your head spins with the need to keep running.

You wear brown plaid Bermuda shorts and a Hawaiian shirt. Sometimes your father's gray trench coat. Your brother wears a red plaid smoking jacket. John, the guitarist, wears a Steve Martin arrow through the head. Todd, the drummer, has a drawing of an asshole (literally) on his bass drum. As soon as you have enough money saved from various jobs you go to Avalanche Studios on the edge of town to record new songs. You perform dressed as Egyptians, The Beatles (circa Sgt. Pepper's), punks, and American tourists run amok. You perfect the art of the silly dance. You play your own compositions (a mixture of Rush, Beatles, Pink Floyd, and Punk—yes, an impossible combination). You openly defy every convention of high school rock bands. And yet—despite this courageous act of rebellion—you lose every battle of the bands you enter but one. The winners: leather clad, long-haired, head banging posers playing covers of Van Halen, AC/DC, Quiet Riot, and Motley Crüe—"Come on feel the noise!" Unconscious parodies straight out of *Spinal Tap,* complete with aluminum wrapped cucumbers in their trousers. Rock on Cleveland! Purveyors of aimless, adolescent rebellion, the kind of rebellion where you are very careful to look and act like everyone else—the kind of rebellion sanctioned in the suburbs because it's a metaphor for the suburbs where acting happy means you are happy. A band that plays a postmodern mish mash of pop and underground culture from The

Beatles to The Butthole Surfers, from Rush to The B-52's doesn't rebel in the "appropriate way." They are not "properly" acting out in codes that can easily be identified. Rock on Bon Jovi! Kick ass, Poison! A formula no different from beige and cream colored houses—no TV or cable antennas showing please! Keep your grass clipped to 2 and 1/2 inches (or we'll have to call the Homeowner's Association), plant your flowers in a row along the porch, leave nothing outside in plain sight. No old cars, rusty cans, shredded tires. And certainly, no detritus.

Your band is all detritus. You're not great. In fact, you're barely passable. And yet, your very existence is a heroic act. Your workshopping sessions in the basement (yes, you know the cool words) keep *The Carol Burnett Show* from the TV upstairs at bay. And now your dad wears a hearing aid, and you wonder if it's the result of all those years of rock and roll pounding up through the floor, all that detritus filling his house, sliming out into the neighborhood.

Looking back, it doesn't escape your notice that this is just another of the many parts you played. The high decibel-level another way to keep the minotaur out. The impossible mix just another labyrinth. But fuck all that. Your amp goes to eleven.

Not even under torture will you admit how many hours you spend exploring caverns, trudging through dark, dank hallways, battling red dragons, blue dragons, green dragons, and black, Frost Giants, Stone Golems, Zombies, skeleton armies, Lichs, Werewolves, Vampires, Orcs, and Goblins, Catoblepas, Cockatrice, Gryphon, Roc, Medusa, Harpies, Succubi, Drow, Githyanki, Githzerai, Death Knights (your personal favorite), and even a giant crab. You'll never understand whether the game is an escape from suburbia or the epitome of suburbia. And for that reason, like a recovered alcoholic, you don't talk about your daily need to enter other worlds, to create campaigns complete with hand drawn colored maps of uncharted regions. You own the original three-volume paperback set of rules published in 1974 by TSR. You don't yet know it will become a franchise, a mega-corporation, a household name associated with moral decline, Satanism, witchcraft, murder, and suicide. You can't yet be aware that future editions of the Dungeons and Dragons trademark will remove all suggestive artwork and references to demons and devils. (You've got to makes sacrifices if you want to become a billion dollar industry!) Even after a few beers with close friends, you'll never describe how the games would begin at five in the evening with pizza and Coke, then go on all night fueled by stale donuts and more Coke only to crash at eight or nine the next morning. Then sleep through the next day—vampires rising at night to start the hunt over again. And not even on your deathbed, not even as you painfully suck in your last gasp of air, will you confess that you started the Dungeons and Dragons club at your high school. Remember the red-haired kid who talked to himself and carried around a copy of *The Necronomicon,* which hid the dagger he palmed, the dagger he flashed one day when you threatened to kill off his character? Or the other kid, the handsome one all the girls liked, who took you into his room in his basement and showed you the altar to Satan he'd made, the altar on which he kept the dolls for people he wanted to hurt? You understood then that though Dungeons and Dragons was your escape, some of its doors led places you'd rather not go. And you remember wondering as you emerged from your friend's basement how many dark dens existed below the carefully manicured surface of your world.

You're twenty-five and Colorado is not big enough to hold you. You want the world, and your first stop is Los Angeles. You tell your fiancée you have to move to where the fencing is—that means New York, Los Angeles or San Francisco. But you can't stomach New York. Never could. So, it's off to the land of surf and sun. The manager of the club in L.A. says you can stay with him if you help out around the club—a little painting and repair work. It's fine by you. And your fiancée says she understands. Deception works equally well in fencing and in life. And if the fencing club is your life, then the manager watches over your body and Stella cares for your soul. Dressed in knee high boots and black leather mini-skirts, with eyeliner as thick as her accent, Stella is your high priestess—and you worship at her feet each and every day.

LESSON THREE: STELLA

"You are nothing," she says. "Nothing but cold water!" She hits you hard across the arm with her sword. "Look at you," she says, circling now. "You stand proper, like English king. Do you want me to bring you fruit, your highness?"

You plant your feet, bend your knees at precisely forty-five degrees, sword arm straight. And you do not answer.

"You don't know what it means to fight," she continues. "Young American from Colorado. Parents take good care of you, no? Never need to fight for anything." She takes your blade in her palm, pulls it into her chest. "Hit me here!" she commands. The steel bending as she impales her chest upon the point.

You stand stock still, connected to her by the blade, the tension in the steel arcing through your arm. "Hit me," she repeats. You pull back your arm to the proper *En-garde,* the position Henri spent years drilling into you. Classical French. "Hit me harder!" she yells. You thrust as hard as you dare. Your eyes lock as the point connects with her chest, and you don't need to hear what she says next. You already know, can see it reflected back in her eyes. She grabs the blade at the peak of its arc, holds it taut so you know what the force of a good hit feels like, then tears it from your hand and throws it against the wall. She steps forward, leans into your ear. "You are no man," she whispers. "I only work with men."

You should go back to Colorado. Champion of the seven state Rocky Mountain region should be enough for you. You can be proud of that. But you don't. Instead, you show the club manager the welts up and down your arms and legs from where she hit you with the side of her blade to correct your position, and you laugh. You tell him she will change everything about your fencing. (She will change everything about you.) And you welcome it.

"You think you can win with strength and speed?" Stella's hand, like a spider, moves up your arm. "You are strong man, yes. I can feel that." She pauses, her hand caressing your shoulder. "You are big man, yes."

She steps back into *En-garde*. Thrusts without warning. You pick up the blade in prime as she's taught you to do. An unorthodox move. Henri would never approve. She disengages and completes the thrust into your chest. You swipe nothing but air. "Strength and speed win kiddy tournaments," she says. "If you want to fence with men, disguise intent. Now hit me!"

You lunge hard and fast. Six parry, coupe and the flat of her blade slams down on your shoulder. You wince from the pain. "Hit me, hard!"

Again you thrust, but this time you pull back your foot, slow down the lunge. She retreats, and when you fumble in recovering the distance, she beats your blade away and swats your arm. Another welt.

"You are nothing but cold water, Peter," she says. "I want hot water."

"I *am* hot water," you say.

"No. Cold."

You say nothing.

"That's very nice," she says, grabbing your blade. "You think you can take anything don't you?" She moves in, strokes the blade in the cup of her palm as she talks. The sensuality of the gesture is not lost on you. "You'll let anyone beat you." She brings her face in close. "Let anyone hurt you." Her mouth inches from your ear. Her breath hot upon your neck. "Nice American," she whispers. "Afraid to hit. Afraid to tell me what you think of me."

Still, you say nothing.

Her finger traces figure eights beneath your ear. "Make lunge short, but fast," she says. "Must look real even if you can't make it real. Gauge opponent's defense. Then follow with straight feint."

She presses her cheek against yours. The rush of blood sears. "When opponent attempts to parry, deceive."

She releases your blade and advances, pushing you backward, taking slow, gliding steps to steal the distance. But you are wary. You keep your guard, matching her rhythm, then breaking it. You move together, two dancers, or better two coupling dragonflies, each fighting to take control of the flight.

"Now build off feint deceive," she says, upping the tempo. "Give opponent what he expects, then take away." She attacks hard to your flank. You parry octave and counter, taking advantage of the moment to push her back with a ballestra. But Stella is a veteran who has faced the pressure of countless world championships. She makes a double tempo retreat, her legs like an insect's. You chase after her. "No!" she screams, hitting you hard across the thigh. You clench your foil, start to stand, to walk away. But then, just as quickly, your knees bend to perfect right angles, your arm sets in position; you dig yourself in.

"Good," Stella says. "The king comes down from his throne."

The club is decorated with photos of champion fencers and movie stills from swashbuckling epics. Errol Flynn fighting in *Captain Blood, The Sea Hawk,* and *The Adventures of Robin Hood.* They even have a bust of Ralph Faulkner. You only recently learned that Flynn didn't do most of his own fighting. His stunt double and fight choreographer Ralph Faulkner turned him into a screen legend.

After your lesson with Stella, you take off your sweat-soaked t-shirt, peel off your knickers and sit for a moment to catch your breath. Sweat rolls down your face as the bust of Ralph Faulkner stares back at you. You can't seem to recover. In fact, the longer you sit, the more sweat beads on your back, your chest, your face. The legend behind the legend looks on, threatening to expose you for the fraud you are. You can feel it.

Drugs mean weakness. No one does drugs. Not your friends, and certainly not you—until the day you and your brother walk to your friend's house to see if they will help you film your 8mm stop-motion remake of Ridley Scott's *Alien*. It's the summer of nineteen seventy-nine, and you're fifteen—old enough to know better. And here's where the memory gets fuzzy. Do they let you into the house? Do you walk up the stairs wondering what that smell is? Do you enter their room through the smoke only to find them acting strange, talking about 'shrooms and making fun of you for being so straight? That's the way one memory plays out. In the other, you never go inside the house. They won't even open the door, and when you call up to them, they shout at you to go home from the window. No matter. You and your brother say you don't need them to make the movie. You talk about set designs and lighting all the way home, but inside you wonder when everything changed, when your world slipped out from under you.

In high school you're rarely invited to the parties. The man in the white shirt—that's you. White because your mother bought you five white shirts (one for each day of the week) for the first commercial you did. White because after the freshman musical (in which you starred) a talent scout who was looking for the next Donnie Osmond came to talk with you and eventually signed you. She promised you would be a star. You tried out for Coppola's *The Outsiders*, but the casting director didn't even let you read. She took one look at you and said you weren't tough enough. Then you tried out for that TV series *James at Sixteen* (at least that's the title you remember), but you were so awkward in the bedroom scene before the camera, talking to that girl about the best way to put on the rubber, that you knew you had no shot.

The new Donnie Osmond is left on his own. He courts loneliness. Isolation is his M.O. So, by the time your senior year rolls around and most of the parties involve drugs or alcohol, you steer clear. Remember, "Just Say No." That's not to say you don't go to some of them. You do. What does it matter if you sit in the armchair in the corner of the living room (every house had an armchair, usually a lazy boy that swiveled) and watch your friends laugh at jokes you don't find funny. Of course, every party's the same. Like some quantum observer who changes the scene just by watching, your presence changes everything: the game being to see who can get you to have a drink or take a hit. Sometimes they laugh about it, other times they become angry, taking your refusal as an indictment. You tell them you are so fascinated with what your mind thinks up sober that you can't imagine an artificial ride as being better. But that's not entirely true. You don't like to lose control, do you?

You call them shadow memories because they flicker in and out of the dark recesses of your unconscious, inchoate. There is a reason for that. The mind must protect itself. It's not that these are repressed memories of traumas—this is not that kind of memoir. Rather, they are memories of almost selves, branches in the infinite plan, forks where you made your choice and yet, that almost life whispers back to you across time and space, that almost self haunts the person you are, reminding you of the many people you could have been. Late at night, getting in cars with someone who was not part of your normal crowd (not your brother, not your band, not Rob or Greg or John) and driving out to a field somewhere—you were never sure how you got there. Sixteen and seventeen year olds throwing beer cans on the ground even as they reach for another. Cigarettes like fireflies flitting through the night. And fights. Always fights in these shadows. Two drunk boys swinging at each other: "Fuck you, you faggot!" while the crowd gathers round. Sometimes couples get out of their cars to watch—mostly not. Drunk adolescents in the back seats of cars releasing their own repressed desires.

And then the ride home. You know he shouldn't be driving. You tell him he's going too fast for a dirt road, and he calls you a fag. The next moment you spin out, crash through a fence and stop inches before someone's living room. You don't remember how you got home.

And then there's the time you spend the night at your other friend's house—let's call him Kevin. You wake to the warm sensation of his hand on your crotch, the swelling as he traces patterns over your underwear. Memory blurs. Do you roll over, ignore the whole thing and wake up the next morning as if nothing happened? Or do you lie there next to him as his hand massages your penis through your underwear? Do you think about how good it feels? Do you?

The further back you go, the more shadows you find. You catch glimpses beneath the surface of memory: Kids alone in their house sniffing glue. Do you want some? Another takes a baseball bat to a parked car. Do you join him? Another tells you to distract the clerk while he steals the Dungeon Master's Guide. Do you go along? Another pulls down his pants and asks you to suck his dick. Do you? Another hits a defenseless kid. Calls a kid a faggot. Calls a kid a queer. Do you stop them? Many, many kids drinking, taking shrooms, smoking pot, disappearing in rooms. Images flash through your mind, but strangely your part in these memories remains in shadow. Flicking in and out like the old TV show *The Outer Limits. Don't adjust your vertical hold. There's nothing wrong with your television set.* You stand on the edge of memory, always observing, wondering when, how, if ever, you participated.

Maybe you don't remember because the television static of the suburbs erases any aberrant behavior. No one talks over the static. You don't talk even when your friend wrestles you to the ground (he's a better wrestler than you because he's on the high school team) and looks at you in a way that makes you squirm. You don't talk about the fact that several of your friends are gay—though in 1980 who had the vocabulary to talk about it. And what would you have said given the vocabulary? You don't talk about the friend who is hospitalized for depression or the parents of friends who are hospitalized for depression or the parents of friends who are gay. Or the friends who commit suicide. Or the parents of friends who commit suicide. You don't talk about how some parents never seem to be around while others are around all the time, following their children to the bathroom where they even flush after them.

This is a test of the Emergency Broadcast System. This is only a test. The broadcasters in your area, in voluntary cooperation with the Federal, State, and local authorities, have developed this system to keep you informed in the event of an emergency. If this had been an actual emergency, the attention signal you just heard would have been followed by official information, news or instructions. This concludes this test of the Emergency Broadcast System.

Switch channels, it doesn't matter. The same high-pitched ring. Check the schedule, see what's playing later. The same message flashes across the screen.

It's a storybook wedding. You ride in a horse and buggy to the downtown Denver cathedral. The crowd cheers as you step forth in your tux and tails, your bride to be in her flowing taffeta gown. The catholic service is long. Not what you want. Not what your mothers want. But what your grandparents want. It's over. Your fencing friends line the steps to the cathedral, swords crossed to make an arch. You walk through. Smile. Wave. Drop exhausted in your hotel bed after. Take a bath. Work to get it up so you can say you actually did it, then fall into a three-year sleep.

"Oh shit," he says when you walk in the door of the Halberstadt Fencing Club on South Van Ness in San Francisco. You've fenced him before, the last time in the third round of the national championship just two months ago. He threw his mask half way across the gym after that bout, followed by his foil. Black card. Kicked out of the tournament. Nothing new for this former college football player, who understood the importance of intimidation to the game. And it looked like the game was afoot.

"If it isn't John Denver," he says. "The country boy all the way from Colorado."

You smile as if he's an old friend. What else can you do? "Good to see you, too."

You shake hands, size each other up.

"Word was you were moving to L.A.?"

Despite his greeting, you think maybe he's excited to see you. Maybe.

"No," you reply. "The coaching's better there, but the fencing is better here. And I need bout experience." You don't mention how complicated things got with Stella.

In a fencing club, tensions follow the rhythms of the season, getting higher as tournament time approaches. By the time of the national championships, fights erupt every night. People hardly speak to one another. Then, after a month vacation, the season begins again, and with it, friendships renew.

You arrive the summer of 1991, the year before the Barcelona Olympics, the year the tension heats more quickly than usual and stays white hot. At first, you break into a sweat every time you pack your fencing bag. Sometimes, you even come up with excuses for not going. You barely see your wife. (Yes, after you returned from Los Angeles you married. A month later, you drove out by yourself to San Francisco where your wife would join you.) You're tired from work. But then, like any animal, you adapt. At first, you watch. Touché!

The Call. Masks fly off. Swords hit walls, jab into the wood floor. *Bullshit!* Soon, the electricity that charges the club charges you. You scream after each touch, then set back in for the fight—your new *En-garde* a mix of what Stella and Henri taught you. You're a cool killing machine. You yell but you never lose it. Not like the rest of them. At least until the night you start to beat Roman, the current national champion.

You ask your new coach, Saul, to ref.

"Don't get me mixed up in your shit, Peter," he replies. "I don't want to ref this bout." And he turns back to the lesson he's giving one of his beginners.

"Come on, Saul," you push. You want him because he's been at the top, and because he's from Bolivia and doesn't take shit from anyone.

"I got a lesson here," he says as he marches the student down the strip.

Roman doesn't seem to care much until he's left waiting with no one to fence. "Look around man," he shouts, finally. "Who else we going to get?"

Saul stops his march. Takes off his mask. "Okay, but I don't want to hear shit from either of you."

"*En-garde,*" he shouts, and Roman puts on his poker face just before his mask goes down. You raise your blade. Set your feet.

"*Allez!*"

Half step advance like Stella taught you, leave the back foot behind in case Roman counters. He does. Parry quarte and a riposte to the shoulder, touché. You have his attention. He slaps the floor with his blade and returns on guard.

Saul shoots you a look, but you can't tell if he's impressed or pissed. Then he shouts again: *"Allez!"*

Roman's next attack is as beautiful an attack as you've ever seen—slow, small advances, accelerating like a bird taking flight, presenting his blade, then withdrawing it as the rhythm of his feet changes. He's teasing you, and you take the bait. *Touché* Roman. Suddenly, you're aware that the others have stopped fencing. Saul shakes his head. And you finally understand: he's trying to make a name for himself as a coach and this isn't helping.

"Allez!"

You attack with a fury: beat double advance, pause. Raise your blade ever so slightly. Engage circle six, ballestra lunge. Let him parry. Give him your back. Take the blade in five and ram it home.

Saul glances toward the door.

The first half of the bout resembles more a dance than a fight as each of you not only tries to score, but also to show how good you can look making the touch. Roman takes advantage of your tendency to rush, finding the space between the beats in your heated assaults to make a quick thrust. But you're determined.

Fourteen to thirteen your favor. Unaccustomed to being behind, Roman makes a mistake, falls into your eight line. You parry and riposte. Realizing his error, Roman continues and sneaks in the touch to your flank. You have the parry. The rules indicate it is clearly your touch.

"Roman's point," Saul says, looking you right in the eye.

"What!" you rip your mask off.

"Fourteen up," gaze still locked on yours.

"Fuck you, Saul!"

The club goes quiet. You feel it, know you are going to regret this moment. "Fuck you," you shout again. That's fucking bullshit."

"*En-garde,*" is all he says. His hand marking the center of the action.

You hear them whisper in the background. *He lost it. He finally lost it. I never thought it would happen.*

The bout continues, but none of the previous elegance remains. The dance has been reduced to a simple fight for survival, and Roman is a survivor. Your moves are too big, too complex for this stage in the bout. He closes the distance and ducks with a straight thrust to your chest. *Touché.*

Roman doesn't even shake your hand. But after, long after, when everyone else goes home, Saul puts his arm around you and laughs. You want to tell him to fuck off again. You probably do. But he keeps on laughing in that way of his. "We're going out for a beer tonight," he says. "And tomorrow, I'm teaching you to street fight. Man, don't they have streets in Colorado? In Bolivia, you learn to fight before you learn to walk."

1 a.m. Saul bought the first round and you bought the second. Now you sit alone in your Honda Civic at the top of Hyde staring down into the fog creeping in over the city. You drive down through the mist. Lower the window. Stick your head out and take the moist air into your lungs. At the bottom, you sit at the stop sign and wait. No other cars on the street. No people anywhere. Let the fog roll over you. Sink down in your seat, wrap yourself in the thick, wet blanket and don't emerge for a hundred years.

LESSON FOUR: SAUL

"You fucked up, Pete," Saul says, putting his arm around you, walking you down the strip in that way he has that shuts out the rest of the world. Then. *En-garde.*

Pris de fer, advance. Coupe. Lunge to flank.

"No, Pete," he says, pushing your blade lower with his hand. "You sneak around the blade. Like this. See. No matter if I parry you still sneak under."

Your legs burn in the lunge. "What happens if the guy sweeps seven, coupe to the back?"

"Try it," is all he says. Soon you're in the position of the teacher, pushing and pulling him through advances and retreats. The cue to attack. Saul takes the blade, advances with a lunge to your flank. You sweep the blade in seven and coupe. Saul recovers forward from his lunge, standing up into you, pulling his blade back and thrusting to your belly. Your own attack falls through the air.

"See Pete, you think like rules, you fence like rules. Remember. It's a knife fight."

San Francisco, Richmond District: Two months after your wedding day. Your wife works in the Stanford cancer clinic. You in a bookstore for now. Later the armory. But that doesn't matter. What matters is your schedule. Tuesday and Thursday from 7pm until 11pm Halberstadt Fencers Club. Monday and Wednesday from 7pm until 11pm Letterman Fencers Club. Weekends tournaments (often traveling). Early mornings running and/or lifting weights.

Days working. You see your wife for exactly 30 minutes every other weeknight between 6 and 6:30pm. Sometimes you fit in dinner. You often look back at that time and say those years were the best of your life.

1992 Pacific Coast Fencing Championships. You face your own coach, Saul, in the final. Fencing is strange like that. No distinction between coach and student. No such thing as a coach once you're on-strip. Like a rhino, Saul charges, gets the touch and rams into you. He takes the yellow card with a grin. What the hell's he trying to do? Aren't you friends? You don't believe in that "All's fair in love and war crap."

"En-garde. Allez!"

You attack too soon. As soon as you thrust, you know it's a set up. He sweeps the blade in seven, jumps Jordan style in the air and slams the point down on your back. Years later that move will still piss you off.

"Allez!"

Engage six. Coupe. False thrust to chest. Recover, pause. Quick beat fleche to chest. As you charge past, you jam your elbow in his ribs. Back *En-garde,* and you can't believe you just hit your coach. Saul's rubbing his ribs, and you're playing dirty. As you lift your gaze Saul grins, and you know it's war.

Tear the tape with your teeth. Wrap it around your forefinger. One strip. Two. Secure it with two pieces around the wrist. You're an expert now. The only problem is the tape no longer keeps back the pain. Two Advils every four hours. What was it your football coach in high school said? *No pain. No gain.* Well, you've got bucketfuls of gain. It's raining gain. But when your opponent beats hard in seven, it's like someone stuck bamboo shoots in your veins. When you sweep the line in six, the pain shoots from your elbow up your arm. Work through it, you say. But what about your knees? Some nights you lie awake worrying if you'll be able to walk up stairs at age forty. No matter. Advil. More Advil.

When you do talk with your wife she asks what you're going to do with your life. You have no answer. All you want to do is fence, you say. For now. But what about later? she asks. You want to ask her what does "later" mean on the fencing strip. There is only now. Always now. But you keep quiet.

LOUISVILLE, 1992:
Again you face the current U.S. National Champion. But this time it's not practice. It's your first North American Cup Final. And you've just taken the lead. One more touch and it's yours. Roman throws off his mask and gets in the ref's face. He storms up and down the strip bellowing and roaring, and you realize only then how afraid he really is. And you know you've got him.

"Êtes vous prêt? Allez!"

He's coming strong so you feed him your blade. He takes it. You step inside, jab him in the ribs. Again, his mask comes off. He's demanding a yellow card for *corps a corps*—body contact. You wait and watch as the young female ref takes it from him. And that's when you start to worry. Why doesn't she shut him up?

Next touch. He attacks. Clean parry one-two riposte. He continues to your chest after your parry. The ref gives it to him even though it's your touch. You bite it back and get *En-garde*. From the sidelines, Saul shakes his head, and you know it's not going to be pretty. All you need is one more touch. Make it clean, you say to yourself. Make it clear. That way there can be no argument. You attack, slow at first to draw the counter, then accelerate. *Touché!* But again, the ref gives it to Roman. "Yes!" "Yes!" he screams. "That's right." And now Saul is in the ref's face. The crowd stirs. They don't understand the calls. But you know what's happening. When it's over, you eat your pride as he shakes your hand and says, "Nice bout."

North American Cup finals: one year later. Nothing's working. You've been fighting your opponent, fighting yourself. But you've scrapped your way in. All you needed was to get in the finals to make the World Team. So why do you let up now? Why do you take the bait with a sloppy lunge into his too big circle six. You could see it coming, but you're tired. Tired of fencing, tired of fighting, tired of your marriage, your life. You almost fall over. He towers above you, celebrates in your face. No matter, you say. You still made the team.

No you didn't. After 4 hours in drug control waiting for the piss to come, when they finally announce the team, your name is not called. You check the list. It can't be. How could you have miscalculated? Too tired to do the math? You missed the team by 5 points out of 2000, the equivalent of one touch out of the entire year. Don't talk to anyone. Pick up your slumping body. Pack up your bag. Go back to your hotel room, and bend over the toilet. Get it all out. Taste the bile as you retch over and over, then lie in your bed and pull the covers about you.

You salute your opponent standing across from you in the grand ballroom of an historic mansion outside Palo Alto. Don your mask. *En-garde.* You attack slower than usual, making each action clear as you were told to do. He responds in kind. The fireplace in the ballroom towers over you. A chandelier far bigger than any you've seen before hangs above. The cameraman sits on a crane circling the chandelier, descending upon you. Keep the action flowing. Pris de fer in four, attack to low line. Let him parry eight. Good. He follows your rhythm. Parry six slow thrust to his head. Make it pretty. Cut.

"I want a shot of your hand next," the director says. You've been here all day filming a commercial for a software company in silicon valley. *We want fencers,* they told you on the phone. *We want something romantic.*

The director explains the commercial will open with only your bare hand as you don your gauntlet. He asks if your hands are callused, and you tell him yes. "Good," he says. "I want it to be gritty, real." But when you take off your glove and he frames your hand in the shot, he pulls back. "It won't work," he says. "You have too many calluses. Your forefinger is knotted with them. It's unusable."

"Okay," you say and back off to eat a sandwich while the director inspects the hands of his crew, looking for the perfect one.

You beg your wife not to apply to med school in Chicago. You ask for one more year. "What do you care?" she asks. "You're gone all the time anyway." But the fencing in Chicago is not as strong, you tell her. What will you do? "You could think about getting a job," she says. "School's going to cost thirty thousand a year—and that's just the tuition." *Don't adjust your vertical hold. There's nothing wrong with your television set.*

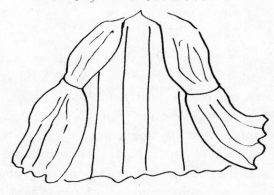

****And Now for a Brief Intermission****

During this interlude, we offer for your reading pleasure the short story:

—All or Nothing at the Fabergé—
(Watch our hero tripping over fiction!)
(Witness the dirty underbelly of the fencing world!)
(You can of course skip reading this story and not miss a thing.)

Roman[1] sees a Parisian skirt decked in green and says he'll meet me[2] in a second. I watch from the side of the strip as he makes his move; he keeps one eye on Johnny and both hands on the skirt. I know what he's thinking. Even though he's two-time national champ and got his spot on the Olympic team locked up, he's still scared of Johnny. And the sad part is he doesn't even know why. Not like me. I'm the one who should be scared. I fence my bout to make the final eight in an hour. Johnny and I both can't make the team. This weekend decides everything. All or nothing at The Fabergé[3]—that's the name of this world cup. The one who makes it the farthest is in. The one who fucks up, well, he doesn't just head for the showers.

You've got to admire the way Johnny walks to the strip. It's not attitude. It's fucking nobility. Like he's the great Shimura—the leader in *The Seven Samurai.*[4] Man that guy just oozed nobility.

I'm waiting for Johnny, pumping him up and thinking how the hell did I get into this insane sport. I'd been a linebacker at USC, but my sophomore year I tore my anterior. The doctor said I should take up fencing to help with the rehabilitation. *Do I look like fucking Cyrano?* I told the doctor. *Fencing.* A half black, half Jap from Watts.[5] *Fencing. Shit!* But, hell, I loved those Errol Flynn movies, so far from Watts.

---

1 Yes, this is the same Roman as on p. 48.
2 Danger: Point of View Shift. Proceed with Caution.
3 Bad cologne, expensive eggs, but a great tournament!
4 Shimura became a model for correct action in our hero's early life—along with Errol Flynn. You figure it out.
5 Through this ethnic extravagance, our hero can get closer to the emotional truth, though he must of course sacrifice objective truth.

The ref prepares to begin the bout. He's Hungarian, though he's dressed like a frog. Damn French, makin' the refs wear tuxes. What do they think this is? *La Cage aux Folles*. Still, I love refs from the eastern block—so open to negotiation. They announce the bout over the P.A. The crowd settles—a few thousand scattered about the stands, not bad for fencing. I'll give the Parisians that much. They've got class, know a good fight when they see one. Johnny and Bianchedi test their weapons, but I'm sticking to the strip.

I make a big show of it. The Hungarian puffs up his neck and pushes me away because I'm right there yelling in Johnny's ear to get nasty. I don't want to leave him. If I leave him, the die is cast, and I'm not sure I want to throw it. But then I see Johnny's dad in the stands, looking tense, even though he's a Vietnam vet. He's my out. I can sit next to him and look clean. I like Johnny's dad, met him the night before. So, I signal Roman, then glance back at the ref to make sure. He nods at me, his eyes closing the deal.

En-garde, s'il vous plaît, the referee says, and Johnny gives him that perfect en-garde, back arm raised above his head, like the tail of a cat on the attack, weapon pointed straight at the opponent's chest, knees bent forty-five degrees. Bianchedi's arms hang down, the point of his weapon drags on the strip. He simply leans forward a bit at the referee's call for en-garde. He's already bouncing. I'm thinking Manolete[6] and the bull.

"*Êtes vous prêt?*" The crowd hushes. The referee raises his hands, then drops them,

---

6 Manolete, another model for our hero—one not easily found in suburban Denver.

"Allez!"

I remember four years ago when Johnny moved from Colorado to San Francisco to train. I hated him.[7] We'd fenced each other on the circuit before. He usually won. I didn't so much mind losing. No, that's bullshit. I hated losing. But, what I hated most was losing to a country boy whose technique and control were better than I could ever hope for. He fenced an upright game: no surprises, no tricks. Totally by the book, and I still couldn't beat him. The only way I could get him was to fence dirty: do the opposite of what a fencer should do. Then, when he got flustered and I was in close, hit him with a cheap-ass move. He didn't understand street fighting. That way I could sometimes win. He hated that. And in a sense so did I. I don't know if Johnny was rubbing off on me or if I was a samurai reincarnated, but I was getting hooked on the purity of the action—you know, the union of mind and body. All that Zen shit. Hell, I even read the old samurai masters, Soho and Musashi. *Sever the edge between before and after.* That's Soho. That's why I never went back to football. How can you compare that to, "No pain, no gain"? Besides, everyone was on the take. Christ, I had friends who spent more time in their BMW's than in the classroom. And it only gets worse in the pros. Sometimes I wonder if my body knew I had to get out of there, if it knew and made it happen. *To know and to act are one and the same.* [8] I don't know who said that, but I know

---

7 In dissociative disorder, formerly called multiple personality disorder, two or more identities or personalities operate. One often exhibits strong feelings toward the other.
8 Compare the two saying for a moment. I give up.

it was a samurai. I'm telling you I'm full of that shit.

"You're the friend I met at the club last night," Johnny's dad says when I sit down next to him. And I've got to think what to say, because my first reaction is *How'd you learn so little about the world?* But I don't. "Yeah, we're teammates," I say.

"Must be tough," he goes on. "Cheering for him on one hand, on the other knowing if he wins it'll affect you." He puts his hand on my shoulder.

"You get used to it," I say. But what I'm not used to is the fact that he leaves his hand on my shoulder for a moment, and I think maybe he really means it.

Bianchedi charges, like I knew he would, his blade low to the ground as he runs, daring Johnny to attack. Johnny lunges straight to Bianchedi's chest, and it looks like he's taken the bait. But it's only a half-lunge. Bianchedi stops on a dime, whips his blade to sweep the line and knock Johnny's blade away from his chest, but Johnny deceives the attempted parry and finishes his lunge. Finta in Tempo. Pure Shimura!—Like when he went into that hut alone to face the crazy thief.[9]

Oh shit! What are you doing here? That's the first thing I said to Johnny, when he arrived at the club down in the mission district of San Fran. *Ladies and Gentleman, if it isn't John Denver.* He hated when I called him that. So I still do. The thing that got me was he just smiled when I said it. Then he put his arm around me and said

---

9 Our hero has often asked himself if he could do the same.

how glad he was to be there and train with the best.[10] So, Roman and I decided we'd fuck with him a bit. Roman did it by beating him every chance he could, and while I couldn't always beat him, I could at least show him what it meant to fence with the men, you know an elbow here, a knee there, maybe sometimes slap him with the flat of the blade across his back. Shit, two years of college ball taught me something. But the boy just kept coming back for more. And the crème de la crème was that he kept getting better. Pretty soon Roman wasn't winning all the bouts. And that's when things got ugly.

Don't get me wrong, Roman wasn't a complete prick. He's just a bit insecure underneath all that bravado.

The crowd roars. *L'attaque pas de droit, touché*. Bianchedi pulled that one out of his ass. "Come on Johnny," I yell. "Your game!" Johnny's dad is yelling too. His dad seems nice enough, not like one of those vets with post-traumatic stress. Couldn't blame that on my old man. He was only stationed in Japan back in the early '60's, didn't actually see combat. I got to hand it to Johnny's dad, flying all the way to gay Paris to see his son. You don't see that too often. Still, I got *doerai* respect for my mom, even if she didn't want me to fence: a Japanese woman raising two kids on her own in the hood.

Don't be like your father, she'd say when I'd skip school. And though I loved her I wanted to hit her. Instead, she hit me. Told me I was running out of chances. She was right. I don't get another shot. I'm thirty. I got in this game late like I said, and I need an Olympic medal to set me up for a nice cushy college coaching job. Maybe I'll

10 When faced with hostility, kindness weighs our hero down. Odd behavior for a fencer, or any athlete. I don't understand why, and it hasn't always served me well. I wish I were different.

get me some coed booty then, too.

Bianchedi's moving the second the ref signals the action to begin. It's like he doesn't know how to retreat. Johnny retreats matching the speed of Bianchedi's attack, then at the last moment he jumps back in double time, extending his arm. Bianchedi slaps Johnny's blade to the ground and lunges to Johnny's chest. The impact is hard; the blade practically snaps.

"What just happened?" Johnny's father grabs me, almost tearing my arm off.

"Bianchedi's touch, if you call that a touch. It's five to three for him."

"The Italian looks like he's insane."

"Crazy wops. No, Bianchedi is good. He's still pissed from being kicked out last year. He's got something to prove. I'd say his style is unorthodox, but I don't even know if he has a style. He'll hit you from anywhere though."

"Can Johnny take him?"

"He'll take him," I say. "But, it ain't going to be easy. Bianchedi's the antichrist."

The father has the same long, pretty-boy eyelashes as Johnny. The same blue eyes. Both of them looking too skinny and delicate to be in the military. I asked Johnny once what the hell he was in the Rangers for anyway. *Cause my dad was a Ranger*, was all he'd said, as if that explained everything. That's the way Johnny was. He assumed things worked a certain way. That if you acted with respect the way your old man raised you, if you busted your ass, you'd succeed.[11] And

---

11 I ate that stuff up, oh did I.

Johnny'd busted ass. Took his master's in Russian from Stanford last year. He was supposed to start his tour with the Rangers right after that, but he asked for a year off to make the Olympics and they gave it to him.[12] He never once doubted that he would make it. He believed it, had seen it in his head every day, and knew it would be so. My world doesn't work that way.

He's fencing Bianchedi so close. That's pure belief. You've got to know you're invincible to fence him that tight. Now it's Johnny's turn to make invitations. He's dropping his point, giving Bianchedi the opening. Bianchedi's wary. He makes a feint, but Johnny fakes the parry four, Bianchedi attacks, Johnny makes his real parry and scores to the flank. Sometimes I admire him so much it hurts.[13]

His dad stands and cheers. I see Roman yelling encouragement over his shoulder to Johnny, but then turn his back, focusing only on the skirt. Roman's already in the final tomorrow. He beat Pavlovitch. I didn't see the bout, but I heard the Russian rolled over for him. Roman's a natural for the sport—all ego and two hundred proof killer instinct. Without that, why bother fencing. Just go into curling or speed walking or something. I won't even mention bowling. If that ever becomes an Olympic sport, I'll quit.[14]

There's got to be anger, or why fence? Anger at a father who

---

12 Okay, Johnny clearly represents one cloak of our hero, but the circumstances of Johnny's life were taken from one of my teammates. That teammate went on to be deployed in the former Yugoslavia, Iraq, and Afghanistan. I have since lost touch with him.

13 More evidence of a dissociative disorder. Many personalities tend to interact with and even admire other personalities.

14 It's currently a sport in the Special Olympics and has strong support for full Olympic status, at least in the U.S. Really.

ran out, or at a hugs and kisses father like Johnny's, or like Roman, angry at the world. They say the only thing in sports faster than the point of the blade when a fencer attacks is a bullet fired from a gun. No time to think. My guess is that's why we all do it.[15]

My problem is now I've got too much time to think. Too much time 'til my bout starts. I can watch Johnny's bout, then warm up for awhile, but I don't like sitting still. Don't like it at all.

There's a flurry of touches. Bianchedi muscles his way in with a bind. Johnny fights back, lunging low and wide as Bianchedi jumps in the air, spread eagle fashion and thrusts, landing a counter just below Johnny's neck.[16] I'm watching, but I'm not seeing it, like Soho's story of the monk stuck in the mud—I can't let go. I smell that sick formaldehyde smell of the hospital, that smell that never covers up the real smell of decay, only mixes with it to make the spit grow thick in your mouth. I see Momma laid out in that hospital bed after her stroke three months ago[17], and I hear my sister Kay's words, *You need to think about our family.* I am thinking about our family I want to tell her, I would tell her if she were here, that's why I'm doing this, to get us all the hell out. But she's not here, never could be here even if we were another family, cause she's at home taking care of

---

15 What am I angry about? Please email your thoughts to the author. His email address is on his website: www.brothersgrandbois.com

16 A real crowd pleaser if done correctly.

17 Taking into account the fact that our hero has thankfully never had the misfortune of visiting his sick mother in the hospital, the above seems a fairly elaborate construction for what is essentially back-story. I'm really just trying to deal with my own feelings of selfishness for investing so much time in what is clearly a meaningless and anachronistic sport. (*Spoiler Alert*) After all, it did cost me my first marriage.

Momma now.

"Did you see that move Bianchedi just threw at Johnny?" Roman's back in the stands now, sitting next to me, pretending he's interested in the bout. "He invented a new parry for that one. Jesus Christ. What's the score?"

"I don't know," I say. "I hear the Russian gave you a present. That was awfully nice. I don't suppose Bel will do the same." I give Roman a knowing look.

"Hey, he needed the money." Roman says, keeping his voice low. "And he wasn't going to make the Russian team anyway. They've already picked their team. Two hundred dollars can buy a lot of Rubles."[18]

"But you didn't need the bout. You've already got your spot."

"I've still got to let them know who's boss," he says, giving me that slick-shit grin. "Now Bel's a different story. Besides the French don't take bribes."

"No."

"Maybe you'll get lucky with the ref."

"Maybe."

"But, I suppose you wouldn't do it anyway. Cause you want to be like him," he says, pointing to Johnny.

"Shut up."

"Just telling it like it is." Roman laughs.

"Shut the fuck up."

---

18 Anyone questioning whether or not cheating actually occurs in international athletics has clearly spent his or her time on more important pursuits than the sporting news. For a quick lesson, simply turn to the Tour de France, any Olympic Ice Skating event, or that favorite American pastime, Baseball.

But all Roman does is flash his smile. "What did you think of that Parisian piece?"

"Not bad," I say. "I'll lay five to one you don't get no booty tonight though."

Johnny glides down the strip, changes tempo to throw the Italian off, then a double disengage.

"That a way, Johnny!" his dad yells. "Eight to seven for Bianchedi, but Johnny's gaining."

I nod my head.

"You know I don't party the night before the finals," Roman says.

"What do you care, you're already on the team?"

"It's a pride thing."

"Yeah, sounds like you bought the Russian with your pride."

"It's all part of the game, man."

"Yeah, all part of the game," I say, but suddenly I don't want to think about the game, I don't want to watch Johnny, or focus on my next bout. I'm feeling like some fat Sumo wrestler is sitting on me, and I want to call the whole thing off. But I can't. And Roman won't shut up.

"Hey, maybe tomorrow night, after I win, we'll hit the Latin quarter, and we can find that ugly bitch again." Roman laughs. But my stomach feels like it's trying to crawl out of me. Like it doesn't want to be part of me anymore. "Don't worry, if we find her again, I'll share with you." Roman's always trying to be buddy buddy with me. But he doesn't know shit. He lost his older brother in a drive by nine years ago back in the Bronx[19], and now he wants me to be his older brother. He doesn't know that his presence makes me want to run from myself, that I usually want to hit him, except I don't and that's the part I hate. Like two nights ago when we were at that bar, I don't even know what it was called and couldn't get there again if you asked me; I just know it was somewhere in the Latin quarter.

Omnes is the greatest fencer ever, Johnny said, taking a swig of beer.

Bullshit! You like him because he fences like a king with a poker up his ass, Roman laughed at his own joke, *Mathias Behr rocks! Omnes was lucky he didn't have to face him in Barcelona.*[20]

You like him because he's German, I said. *Roman, how come you got a name like Roman and yet you're German?*

Roman is a German name, asshole.

Doesn't sound it.

Roman got all fidgety, swirled the beer around in his glass, then took a big swig. *My parents wanted to get away from Germany, but they didn't want us to lose our heritage. That's why I got the name. It was a compromise. It's German but it doesn't sound German.*

Maybe they should have named you Cicero or Seneca, Johnny said.

Shut up! Roman shifted his gaze to the bar where a homely looking girl sat by herself. *I think I found us some company. I'm*

---

19 This would make a great movie.
20 Philippe Omnes was gold medalist in the 1992 Barcelona Olympics. But the greatest fencer in history was probably Alexander Romankov (5 time World Champion), with Christian D'Oriola, and Sergei Golubitsky also in the running.

going to have a little fun.

Leave her alone, Johnny said, trying to grab Roman and missing as Roman dodged out of the way.

Gentlemen, this is Claudette, Roman made an exaggerated bow, keeping one arm around Claudette's waist. *She doesn't speak English.*

That's great Roman, since between the three of us we can barely ask where to take a crap in French, I said. Johnny wasn't laughing.

I know more than you think, Roman said. Then to the girl, *Voulez vous boisson?*

She giggled to herself and nodded.

Roman signaled the waitress for a drink, then, smiling, turned to the girl, *You sure are an ugly bitch aren't you?* He kept the smile on his face and nodded appearing as if he was the girl's best friend.

Oui, said the girl, smiling back.

I laughed along with Roman.

Stop it, Roman. Johnny shifted his glass to my side of the table. *It's not funny.*

You're so ugly, Roman continued, *and you think I'm interested in you. That's really pathetic.* His voice was soft and sweet.

You're pathetic, Roman. Johnny's tone was unmistakable.

The girl glanced nervously between Roman and Johnny, unsure what was happening.

What did you think a guy like me would see in you? Roman said, still smiling at her. *Maybe if you're lucky, I'll take you out back, in the alley, stick my fingers in you...*

Johnny jumped at Roman. Beer splashed over the girl. She stepped back, covering her face. The glass shattered on the floor, as Johnny threw Roman over the table. They fucked around, each trying to pull away enough to land a punch. *Why would you do that?* was all Johnny kept saying in between the grunting and yelling of *you asshole,* or *you fucker.* I stood watching, kind of curious as to who would win. In fencing, Johnny was technically better, but he didn't have the killer instinct the way Roman did. And I wanted to see if Johnny had it now. He did. He landed a punch to the side of Roman's head when I pulled him off.[21]

You're gonna fucking break your hand before the tournament, I said.

Roman jumped back up and tried to get at Johnny, but I stopped him. Told him he'd been an asshole enough for the night.

He spit. *Just fooling around,* he said. *I wouldn't hurt him. Then he'd have an excuse for not making the team.*

Two angry looking waiters came over and shoved us out the door, yelling. Roman yelled back, *Fucking French! Who wants to fight? I'll fight you, you French faggots.*

Shut up, Roman! Johnny yelled when we were outside.

You don't tell me what to do. Nobody tells me what to do. Roman made another run at Johnny, and I stepped in the way. He stared at me for a moment, then ran off down the street, yelling up at the apartments above the shops that stood closed on the street below. *Come on, you French faggots! Who wants a fight?* He stood in the middle of the street, screaming. *I'll take you all on. Pansy asses! Come on and see if you can take a real American whooping.*

---

21 Compare scene to p. 85 of memoir. Which Latin Quarter scene is true? Hint: In general, Johnny acts as a fictional representation of the way our hero would like to be.

A young couple that had been getting it on outside the bar across the street looked at us like we were gang bangers and ran inside.

Johnny looked at me and shook his head. *The idiot,* he said. *He's going to get himself killed.*

At that moment I felt closer to Roman than I ever had.[22]

Bianchedi is attacking again, his blade moving in front of him like a blender. Johnny's standing his ground. Bianchedi launches, looking like he's going to the high line, but finishing low. Johnny knocks the blade away with a circle six parry just as the point grazes his flank and hits Bianchedi with a one, two riposte to his belly. Score eleven all.

"You're a fucking samurai!" I jump up, yelling. "A samurai!" Roman looks at me like I've gone crazy.

"If he wins, it's not helping your cause," Roman says.

I glance down at Roman. *Maybe I'm different than you*, I want to tell him, but I say nothing because I don't believe it.

Bianchedi digs in, and when the ref says, *"Allez"* he doesn't even lift his point up for the attack. He charges, and Johnny raises his point to Bianchedi's chest. Johnny gets the touch, but Bianchedi doesn't care. The bastard runs straight through Johnny, knocking him to the floor, then kicks him as he passes.[23] I can see the referee reach for the black card in his suit pocket, then hesitate, glance around the arena, and put his hands to his sides. He clasps his hands together

---

22 This is true no matter which cloak our hero wears. Roman's need to fight, to lash out at the world was something I understood all too well.

23 Bianchedi is modeled on a real Italian fencer. I can't tell you who because it would subject me to a slander suit. Oh, what the hell. His name is Stefano Cerioni, the bad boy of fencing.

behind him so that he won't be tempted to draw the card. Johnny's up. He takes off his mask, but stays on the strip. He doesn't yell at refs,[24] but I can hear the tension in his voice, as he asks why there was no warning for *corps a corps*. Body contact, I laugh, if that was just body contact then those police were using feather pillows on old Rodney King. Johnny turns to me in exasperation. I shrug my shoulders and shake my head, like I can't believe the way he just got screwed. *Sorry, those are the breaks, kid*. There's too much riding on this bout. It's not my problem if he doesn't understand.

Johnny puts on his mask, and I can see he's pissed, though for Johnny that means he's going to be coldly efficient. The ref backs away from the strip and calls, "*En-garde!*"

Johnny's dad is asking me what happened. I pretend I'm talking to Roman. But I can't ignore it when he grabs me by the arm again. He wants to know why the guy didn't get kicked out. What can I tell him? I tell him European refs sometimes let offenses slide because they believe in the purity of combat. They don't want a ref's call to decide a bout, they believe in *mano a mano*. That's what I tell him anyway.

"Johnny ought to get mean then," he tells me.

"He doesn't know how," I say, but I'm thinking, *In Watts we learn to get mean before we learn to walk.*[25]

"It's my fault," he says. "I always told him that if he worked harder than anyone else, if he drilled to the point of perfection then

---

24 A slight exaggeration, as the astute reader is sure to point out. Please refer to p. 49.

25 The author must give credit where credit is due, but dear reader, you already know it was our hero's coach, Saul, who inspired this statement.

he would win."

"He's damn good, there's no question about that. Even Roman here's afraid of him." Roman gives me another look.

"But it's not enough." He rubs his hands together, over and over, in his lap.

When is it ever enough? If I had a fucking clue when it was enough, would I be here now?[26] "It's going to be all right," I tell him. "Johnny can take care of himself."

When I was nine, my momma made me take piano lessons. She'd sit on the bench next to me while I practiced. I remember, when I'd make a mistake, she'd slam the lid down on my fingers. She wasn't big on affection. But I didn't care. Made me try harder. I'd sit and play that damn piano all night just so she couldn't sleep. After awhile she stopped sitting on the bench with me, thinking she'd made her point. That's when I stopped practicing for good.[27]

"Man, Johnny's up twelve to eleven. It looks like you're gonna have to go another round to make the team," Roman says. "I bet you'll fence each other in the final eight." He laughs, even though it's not funny.

Johnny moves him down the strip, accelerating his tempo as he goes, then a sudden burst, ballestra lunge. Bianchedi falls backward to the ground. He's up immediately, and in the ref's face. The ref pulls out a yellow card: *"Avertissement, corps a corps."*

---

26 If our hero had a clue, would I be writing this?
27 Lest the reader think our hero had a bad mother, and thus our hero's mother gets upset and calls him on the phone crying, be assured that his mother was quite wonderful.

Johnny does a double take. He can't believe it. He didn't touch Bianchedi with anything but the point of his sword. He knows it. I know it. The ref knows it. Hell, even Bianchedi knows it. But that doesn't change the facts.

"Where the hell's your coach?" Johnny's father asks. "Can't he stop this?"

"He's the guy in the corner with a hangover,"[28] I say. And I know what Bianchedi's thinking right now. He's thinking put that one away for later. And Johnny's thinking this is not right, and there is no doubt within him.[29]

"Allez!"

Bianchedi scores with a double coupe to Johnny's back. I don't know how he finds the target back there. He's like a goddamn heat seeking missile. Twelve to twelve.

Johnny fights back with a clean, long attack, his point dancing through the air. Bianchedi ducks, thrusting his weapon blindly in front of him. The trick works.

"Jesus Christ," Johnny's dad says, "Is that legal?"

"It's legal, but it's a low blow." Literally, I think. Now I see where Johnny gets it from. His dad's as bad as he is. My motto is: on the strip, as in life, anything goes. I make a move to leave. I need to warm up for my bout, but then I see Roman lying with his eyes closed on

---

28 This is not meant to be a cheap shot at American fencing coaches. The truth is, the U.S. Fencing Association rarely has money to pay for coaches at international events (or at least that was the case at the time our hero was fencing), and I needed a quick excuse for why the coach was unavailable.
29 Our Hero would like to think that kind of clarity is possible. Perhaps that is another reason why I write.

the bleachers next to me like he couldn't give a shit and something in me clicks. "Kill him," I yell, and Johnny's dad looks up at me.

"Too bad he couldn't make it here."

Johnny's moving in and out like a boxer. "Stick him!" I yell, not able to control myself, and wonder what the hell is in my head. Is this all an act? But I don't know what part of me is the act, and I can't help feeling the thrill as I watch Johnny stick and move. And I see, without looking, the way in which Johnny's father arches his neck, breathing deeply, yet never getting enough air to ease the anxiety. And I feel, the sweat on the palms of his hands as he rubs them together, then folds them in his lap. "Stick him!" I yell again.

"I hear your dad was in the military too," Johnny's dad says, almost like he wants to calm me down.

"Yeah."

"Yeah, too bad," I say and flash him that smile again. But this time it's like he can see right through it. He holds me in his gaze, and I sit there and let him.

"We've all got our fights," he says, nothing more than that.

Part of me is pissed off, thinking that's all you got to say. But all I can say is, "He lost his a long time ago." And I turn away.

"Hard to know sometimes if you're winning or losing," he says.

"I know I've lost when I want to hit someone, and I don't like the feeling."

"Nobody does, " he says. And then he smiles, and I can't decide if I feel like hitting him or not, cause I know the smile is real; the goddamn smile is real.

Johnny gets the next point with a blinding attack that evades Bianchedi's defenses. Thirteen up. And suddenly, I'm quiet. I rise and make my way to the gym floor.

They trade touches, fourteen to thirteen Bianchedi, then fourteen up. Johnny used to brag that he never lost a bout at fourteen a piece. And I know what he'll do. He'll stand there arm straight, point aimed at Bianchedi's chest, waiting for Bianchedi to make that big preparation, to sweep the line with that windmill circle parry of his, and he'll deceive Bianchedi's blade with finta in tempo, and lunge sure and straight. And the thing is, I don't care. If he ends it like he began the bout. If he keeps it pure and true, I don't care. In that moment, all I want to see is the feint deceive. I want to see Bianchedi try to stop as he impales himself on Johnny's point. I want to see the arrow line of Johnny's lunge, back foot planted in the floor echoing the surety of his mind. I want to see the arc of his blade as it impacts Bianchedi's chest, feel the tension flowing through that arc. In that moment, I want to see a touch that I know I have no chance in hell of ever making. I don't do finta in tempo, never have. I win any way I can, like I said.

The sound of the impact of the point on Bianchedi's chest brings me back, and I know it's all gone the way I imagined. I can see it in the surprised way Bianchedi's body folds up, the way Johnny stands there, both arms outstretched, as if inviting the world to partake in the moment with him. But then Bianchedi falls down. He rolls around a couple times rubbing his thigh before standing up and limping about the strip, yelling, demanding a red card.

Johnny'd taken his mask off, but the joy on his face vanishes as he realizes what is happening. The Italian coach steps forward, demanding a red card, but he doesn't need to, the ref's hand is already in his suit pocket. Our coach looks as if his hangover just got worse. I can't watch. I hear Johnny scream "No!"[30]

From where I begin my warm up drills, I can see Johnny in the corner of the gym pacing back and forth, yelling at himself. I think of Musashi, *By knowing form, one knows emptiness.* And I know Johnny's perfect form doesn't count for shit now.

His dad comes over to me, "I don't know what I should do." He looks bad, worse than Johnny.

"Let him be," I say. But really I want him to let me be. I don't want to see his face right now.

We both watch as Johnny slides slowly down the wall until he's sitting on the floor, head and hands between his knees. His back arches and falls abruptly, and we know he's crying.

His dad looks at me again, but I don't look back, "Last time I saw him cry, he was ten years old," he says. "I'd gone into the basement and secretly finished his model airplane for him overnight. I thought he'd be surprised." Then he wishes me good luck and walks to his son. I work through my drills, but I can't stop looking at them: the father standing to the side of the son, knowing there is nothing he can do.

Five minutes before my bout, and my head's a mess. I've got to take a piss. I just get to the urinal and the Hungarian ref comes

---

30 This scene actually took place at the 1992 National Championships in Chicago. But my memory can't be trusted. At any rate, doesn't Paris make a far more interesting location?

up and starts peeing next to me. I can't pee. He looks at me and nods. Transaction completed. He didn't understand English and I didn't understand Hungarian, but it didn't matter: a little American green overcomes all language barriers. Shrugging his shoulders and shaking his head as if to say that was much harder to pull off than he'd counted on, he zips himself up and then stands there. I'm still trying to pee. But I can't cause he's just staring at me, waiting for something, like he wants more. I'm watching my dick, but not a goddamn drip. And now I want to pee more than anything, let it all out, but it won't come. I'm thinking of waterfalls, rivers, faucets, but nothing cause that Hungarian's eyes are glued to my back. And I'm thinking this is a bad sign, you can't fence like this, but the Hungarian's still standing there, so I zip up, turn to him and say the one phrase in Hungarian that I know, *"Baszd Meg!"* Fuck you! And I walk out, but before I do, I see the Hungarian screw up his face as if I'd just peed all over him.[31]

Bel comes to the strip. The ref's an Austrian. He tests our points and I'm still trying to fire myself up, *Come on Al! This guy's a chump.* But nothing's coming yet. I can still see Roman lying on the bleachers across the gym. I put on my mask and shake my legs out, when I see Johnny standing behind the ref. He's looking at me, and there's an intensity in his eyes. I don't want to look back, but then I realize he's not accusing me. He's saying, *Kick the fucker's ass!* Only he's not saying it out loud. He just raises his fist in front of his face shaking it like we're together on this one. And I know he's going to stand there the whole bout, pushing me with those long-lashed blues

---

31 I didn't know Hungarian at the time, but learned it years later.

saying, *Stab the fucker for both of us.* And he's not going to yell a damn thing cause then the ref will kick him off the floor and send him back to the stands.

The ref is calling, *"En-garde,"* and I'm thinking about the time when I helped Johnny move to an apartment closer to the fencing club, since he had to sell his car to pay for his training. I'm thinking about how I wanted to help him. How it felt good to help him because he'd sold his car and now we both had nothing: nothing but fencing. And there was a kinship between us, and I remember wondering if that kinship started that day or if it'd been there all along. Then I see Momma sitting at the kitchen table, staring into me one morning about a month after Dad left. She's saying, *You strange boy. You don't cry for nobody,* and then I'm laughing, though it feels like I'm crying cause it hurts so much, and I'm thinking how funny it is that we so often kill what we love.

Êtes vous prêt?

*PLEASE TAKE A MOMENT TO ANSWER THIS BRIEF QUIZ BEFORE CONTINUING WITH THE MEMOIR:

1. The above is clearly fiction as no one would ever use the word "booty" that often. T/F

2. The above is clearly non-fiction, though the writer has fooled himself into thinking it is fiction as a means of shirking responsibility for a reprehensible act. T/F

3. Fiction and Non-fiction are meaningless labels. (This question requires an essay: 4-5 pages, double-spaced with 12pt font).

4. The whole story is a load of hooey as the author was never really in contention for an Olympic spot. T/F (hint: to answer this question, please look on p. 87)

AND NOW WE RETURN TO THE MAIN ATTRACTION**

LESSON FIVE: JANUSZ

You put on your mask and get *En-garde,* wondering how he'll fold his long blonde hair up inside his own mask when he puts it on.

"No. No masks," he says.

You look around the University of Chicago gym and realize his mask is nowhere to be seen. "What do you mean, no masks?" you ask before lifting your own. "If either of us is off the slightest bit…"

"No masks. In fencing there is no room for error. If you understand in lesson, you will act it in competition."

You set your mask on the ground, wondering if you'll come back for another lesson.

Though you keep your blade aimed at his chest, the first part is only footwork. Slow advances and retreats, setting the rhythm.

"Where are you?"

"What do you mean?"

His double advance catches you off guard. "Where are you on strip?" There is a hint of impatience in his voice. A feint to your low line. Parry eight, riposte. "You need to know where you are in space at all times. Where is your opponent?" Direct thrust to the chest.

You parry but can't return the attack. He's already too far away.

"I know. . . I need to keep good distance," you stammer between breaths, as you attempt to chase him down.

"No!" He knocks your foil away, advancing double time now. "Where is your opponent in space and also in *time*," he shouts as he marches. It's all you can do to retreat and keep the distance. "Where is his head? Is he in the moment? Or has his concentration failed him. That's the moment to strike!"

You hesitate, processing what he's said, but mostly thinking of your exhaustion. A quick ballestra lunge, and he covers the distance you fought to maintain. Your legs refuse to move back another step, so you close the distance with a coupe attack in an attempt to break his rhythm—a cheap shot and you know it. Unbelievably, he retreats. You relax, having gained a moment, and that's when he attacks. All the rest has been a ruse. The lunge is swift and straight to the chest. You have no time to defend yourself. The bruise to your ego far worse than the bruise you are now rubbing on your chest. Janusz extends his hand.

The gold medal match at your first U.S. Olympic Festival. 1993. San Antonio. And you're 5th in the U.S. But today you're the best. Today you haven't lost a bout. The crowd numbers about a thousand—not bad for fencing, despite what George Carlin said. And you can't believe you're here. You can't believe you're fencing for the gold. The cliché is that your life passes before your eyes on the moment of your death. Well, if that's true, then you're dying now. As you walk on strip, the tunnel of light swirls behind your opponent. He's only a shadow. It's the shimmering light that's real, and it pulls you into those memories that wait lurking beneath the murky surface. You fight them away, aim your point at the shadow's chest. But as you take a deep breath, you run through fields, catch lizards, stinkbugs, and skinks. Skate the pipe. Fish the river. Run down the mountain late at night afraid of bears and bats and lightening. Make movies. Make music. Act in plays, one after another. The foghorn calls to you from San Francisco Bay, and you look out from the back porch of your one bedroom apartment, wanting to peer through the fog but not wanting to because it's so different from the blue sky of Colorado. Yes, you secretly want the fog to keep getting thicker. So thick it will stop traffic. So thick it will shut down the city. So thick it will stop the world. And then the referee calls you to *En-garde*.

"*Êtes vous prêt? Allez!*"

Eager to steal the rhythm of the bout early, both fencers attack. You lunge straight, but your step is too big, your thrust too hard. He's coming fast, his blade like a blender. He catches your guard in his as you collide, your hand caught as it twists around, caught as the two bodies slam together. Bones snap.

You drop your foil and grab your hand. It's wrong. Not straight. The broken bones pushing upward against skin. Your first instinct is to push them back together again, and so you do. The sound makes you go woozy. And then the pain comes. By the gasp of the crowd, you're sure it's not good. The blood drains from your face. The referee asks if you need to sit down, and you do. He asks if you can continue, and you say yes. Of course, you can continue. You just need a minute. After that minute passes, you mount the strip once again, take up your foil, but when you try to close your hand around it, your hand doesn't respond. They rush you to emergency, where you sit in the waiting room for what seems like hours next to a Tae-Kwon-Do athlete whose face has been shattered by an errant kick. Suddenly you don't feel so bad.

Later that night, when you return, your hand in a cast, the tournament is over. Your friend—the guy who said "Oh, shit," the first day you walked into the club in San Francisco, is the first to greet you. He hands you the gold medal and tells you they decided to award an extra this time. You smile even as he tells you that he heard the snap of the bones in your hand all the way up in the stands.

Chicago, Oak Park: Two years after your wedding day. 7am. Drive wife to Medical School. 7:45 am. Go to work as a substitute teacher in area high schools and jr. highs, then on to the University of Chicago where you work as Asst. Varsity Fencing Coach. After practice, it's time for your lesson with Janusz. Tuesday and Thursday nights you fence at the club in downtown Chicago. Pick up your wife at the med school between 11pm and midnight. Wednesdays you fence at Northwestern, then pick up your wife. Somewhere in between: lunch breaks, dinner, weekend mornings when you're not fencing, etc. you study for the GRE and the LSAT because though you can't stop moving, you know you are lost, and you think you can find yourself in grad school.

"Peter you need international experience," your old coach, Henri, says over the phone. He came to visit for a week in San Francisco, but he didn't like the fencers, their unorthodox styles, their affect on you. And so you haven't talked in a year. But now, three months into your time in Chicago and you call him. You tell him you don't know what you're doing anymore. "You need to get out of this country," he says. "Go to France. Fence. Meet a French woman, get fucked. It will do you good." You tell him it's impossible. You don't have the money. A week later you open a letter from him with a check inside for five hundred dollars. Probably half his monthly salary as a bagger at the grocery store. You book a flight to your first world cup in Paris.

Through the darkness and smoke, you can barely see your opponents, now teammates, sitting across from you at the table in the back of a bar in the Latin Quarter. There are four of you. The national champion signals for another round of beer, but the waiter doesn't come. He's fed up with these drunken men who talk too loud in English. So, the national champion gets the beer himself. He returns with a French girl. She looks too young to be in a place like this, too alone.

"I found us some company," the national champion says. And for awhile you argue about who is the greatest fencer of all time. Some argue for Romankov (yourself included), others for Numa, for Omnes. But the national champion keeps eyeing the girl as if he's irritated. "You don't say much, do you?" he says. A couple of the guys laugh. *"Oui,"* she says, lowering her gaze. She sips her vodka and water. "I'm going to have a little fun," the national champion says. "You're not very pretty," he says to the girl in a sickly sweet voice. *"Oui,"* she says, nervously sipping her drink. "Leave her alone," you want to say. But you say nothing. The national champion goes on. "You're just ugly, aren't you," he says. "And you probably think I'm interested in you." The girl continues to sip without looking up. "What do you think I could possibly see in you?" he asks. He reaches his hand out, takes the girl's free hand, plays with her fingers in his own. "Look at these stubby fingers," he says in his sweetest voice. The girl laughs, but her gaze shifts to the door. Your teammates laugh, too, then return to their beers as silence settles about you.

Everything in green, that's how you remember it. Green carpet along the pistes. Tables draped in green cloth on top of which are programs handed out by beautiful young women in green skirts and green jackets. Everywhere the smell of Brut. It is after all the 1994 Brut Faberge World Cup in Fencing. Once on the gym floor, you try not to stare at the Russian team made up of former military officers—men who've been training in fencing since they could walk. The only thing more precise than their footwork is the efficiency of their hand. Normally, military efficiency would be an oxymoron. Not here. The Italian team sprawls in another corner smoking feverishly, and yet you know every cigarette focuses their passion. Always concerned with form, the French take lessons until the last possible second. The Germans bout casually in the center of the arena, as if the whole point was to put on a show. And maybe it is. At an average height of six foot six, they make an imposing team. The Americans—a rag tag bunch made up of yourself, Roman, Al, Matthias, the young Peter (You call him Peter Jr. though he's taller than you), and Terence. You've been in Paris a week training and drinking. And now it's time to test your metal.

Your pool consists of the Russian Pavlovich, the young Italian Sanzo, the Frenchman Bel, a Swiss, and a Chinese. A quick tally and you know you and the Swiss are the weak guys. First bout—Sanzo, the Jr. World Champion. He takes you for granted and pushes the attack. Quick parry riposte. Simple. Clean. Your touch. He won't make the same mistake again. The bout swings back and forth until it's tied at four a piece. Sanzo is nervous. He's tallied the pool as well and knows he can't afford to lose to you. You're confident. Never in your wildest dreams did you think you'd be toe to toe with the hot Italian everyone's been talking about. The next great champion. You set him up with a slow attack. Show him the big step. Then pull it back. Keep it small. He lunges hard—full commitment, and you know you've got him. Parry four, riposte. Same as the first touch. You love symmetry. Only somehow, your point doesn't hit home. Did he turn at the last second, flatten himself so that the point slid past. No time to recover. He makes a quick in-fighting jab as he closes the distance. If Saul were here, he would shake his head. Never lose to a cheap touch.

You take out the Swiss next. Then run over Bel, who seems surprisingly sluggish given his reputation. You couldn't even see the Chinese coming. Only three advance to the next round, so it all comes down to Pavlovitch. Not good. Though perhaps you have a chance. He, too, looks sluggish. After the first touch, you realize his "sluggishness" is a ploy. Like a snake, he sneaks up slowly and strikes before you even think to take a step. You score two touches. Not enough. Your first World Cup experience is over. You should be sad. You should brood about it all day, reliving each touch. But you wander the streets of Paris in a state of ecstasy. You tell yourself over and over that this is what you were meant to do. It may be the happiest day in your life. In fact, you don't sleep all night. You replay every touch in your mind, and the smile on your face gets bigger and bigger. Three months later you will leave your wife. Three months after that you'll file for divorce and quit fencing. And though you'll try many times in the years ahead to come back, the feeling will be gone. Lost in the *arrondissements* of Paris, the same way the cul-de-sacs of your youth swallowed over and over each and every moment of ecstasy.

It happens in the car on the way home from the hospital. You stop on the side of the road before your apartment and tell your wife you want a child. Nothing makes any sense, you tell her. And a child would give you focus, meaning. She agrees. And that night in your blue Toyota Corolla you plan out when you'll have the baby, how you'll stay home while she finishes medical school. And then she tells you that you can bring the baby to the hospital for her to breast feed every three hours or so, that way it won't slow down her studies. You can't shake the image from your head. Standing in the hospital hallway, holding your newborn child, waiting for her to get out of class so she can give the child her breast.

The applications for graduate school in English literature arrive but you throw them in the trash. You take the LSAT. Get into a few law schools in the Chicago area—even get scholarships. But you don't go. Instead you go to Chiropractic Day—a day where potential chiropractic students follow actual students through their school routine. You're sitting in anatomy. Front row. The cadaver spread out on the table before you with a sheet over it. They don't show you the whole corpse uncovered. And you are relieved. Instead, they peel away a piece at a time. First the head, a woman's head. You cringe, avert your eyes, but with shut lids, dried and puckered skin, the head has no affect on you. You can do this, you tell yourself. Maybe you'll be a chiropractor after all. Next, they pull back the sheet that covers the foot. Not bad. Almost interesting the way you can see the tendons outlined, the bones. But then they pull back the corner of the sheet that covers the right hand. It lies before you, palm up, fingers spread like a spider. No, the problem is it's not a spider; it's all too human. The deep grooves of the palm, the calluses near the joints, the slight curl of the fingers, the way the pointer curves into the others, and the way the thumb stands alone, separate. You know now why Rembrandt focused his *Anatomy Lesson* on the arm and hand of the thief Aris Kindt. The lead student takes out his scalpel. *This is where we'll begin the lesson*, the teacher says. *With the tendon of the flexor carpi ulnaris. Make the incision just so.* You're going to be sick. You're sure of it. Get up. Run to the exit.

You watch through the office window as she whips around the corner, jerks into the parking space and storms in. Your wife's not mad; she is only late. You introduce her to your co-worker (though it's a temp job you've been there three weeks and so the term "co-worker" seems appropriate). Tanya, the "co-worker," the marketing director, and your boss, stops to talk with your wife, and as you watch the way in which she diffuses your wife's tension—something about the warm angle of her smile, the way she looks at your wife as if she's actually listening, the way she touches her shoulder as she eases into her space—Suddenly, you realize you've made a terrible mistake.

The first time you sleep with your boss, you come home to your wife who is watching your wedding video. She asks if you want to watch it with her, but you don't say anything. The next day you buy a plane ticket back to Denver, tell your wife you need some time. She gives you a week. After that, she says, it's finals.

You sleep on the floor of the studio apartment. No furniture. No blankets, books or CD's. Mid July in Chicago without air, without even a fan. You wake soaked in sweat, to kids peering in the ground floor window. *Look at the naked man!* To pass the time, you often walk to the Lincoln Park Zoo. Spend hours at the gorilla exhibit. Watch them heave feces at each other.

You don't have much. She kept almost everything. The little you do have, you throw away—the photos, the clothes, anything that reminds you of her—toss it all in the dumpster behind your apartment. The three thousand dollar engagement ring, too. (She gave it back.) You hope, sometimes, that the man in burlap who searches through the garbage will find the ring, that he'll find it and know what to do with it. That he'll know more than you.

Dressed in black, Janusz waits for you, tapping his foil against his palm.

"What's more important in fencing, to hit or not to be hit?" he asks after your first phrase.

"To hit, of course."

"No." Double advance, engage in six. *Watch it, your shoulder is exposed.* "If you are hit, it is over. You must learn to think that way. Defend yourself first. That's the most important thing. Then take advantage of opponent's mistakes."

He pushes the tempo of the lesson. You tell your legs to move, but they don't respond today.

"You cannot carry the world onto the fencing strip, Peter."

"I'm fine," you say. And to show him. Pris de fer in six, bind to seven and ram it home. You almost catch him. But he's seen it all. He's done it so long he no longer has to think. His body reacts based on your hand position, and he's out of distance.

"Are you?" Feint deceive to your flank. "Why are you here?"

"What do you mean?" Retreat, feed the parry. Recover with advance and circle six.

"Why are you here?" he repeats, marching you down strip. Ballestra lunge.

"To be the best fencer I can be," you say. Parry. Feint to belly.

"Not running from anything?" Feed parry. Take blade in four, glide riposte with advance.

"No," you say. "I'm just where I want to be." Circle parry. Try to find his blade.

He evades. You cannot stop the thrust.

National team training camp, Palo Alto. You welcome the time away, the chance to think. Or better, not to think. To act. Simply to act. Mornings you run, followed by a lesson and bouting. Lunch. Afternoons, another lesson and more bouting. It's the same every day for two weeks. You're the model. Even with the national champion there, you reign supreme. You can beat him in practice. You can handle them all. But each day the tension rises, fights break out. The national champ begins showing up late or not at all. You follow the other team members through the Stanford Mall, after the coach cancels practice, saying you need a rest. You watch as Matthias uses his quick reflexes to steal cologne. Back to practice.

Allez!

Matthias charges down the strip like a rhino, doesn't even worry about taking your blade and slams the flat of his own blade across your back.

Allez!

Take his blade in four, hold it. Ballestra lunge and ram it into his chest. Make it stick. Next victim.

Allez!

The national champ attacks, but it's all testosterone. You see it now. He tries to run you down, to intimidate with a counter. He gets the first touch. Leans into your mask and screams in your face.

Allez!

He won't hit you again. You know it. Give him the opening. Counter-time. He attacks full bore, and like a land mine you explode with parry four riposte to the flank. Try it again. And again. It won't matter. You hit them all. One after the other. But you can't hold on.

The rest of the fencers go home. You stay late into the night to drill. Arm first, then feet. Small steps. Lunge against the practice dummy. Push your mind into the point of the blade. Lunge again, harder, faster. Just like Stella said. Hit hard. Make the blade bend. Feel the tension of its arc. Then feel nothing. Your opponent is before you. Beat quarte flank, disengage six, riposte with glide to high line.

Desperate to stem the rising tension, the coach announces after morning practice that he has paid for the team to receive massages and a full spa treatment that evening after a steak and lobster dinner. He drives you to the facility and leaves you there. Because you will get massages after, and because none of you wants to seem the prude, you all enter the bathhouse naked. There is a hot tub and a hole full of ice-cold water in the floor big enough for one person at a time. The five of you sit in the hot tub together. Jokes and nervous laughter as you distance yourself from each other, make sure no feet are touching. You take turns daring each other to jump into the cold bath, but no one will do it, perhaps afraid of the effect of the cold water on your privates.

You jump out to the cheers of your teammates, and submerge yourself into the freezing water. Only your head rises above. The shock is so intense you can't breathe. And your teammates laugh. Then, slowly, you sink your head under the water. Keep it there, and you wonder if somehow you could breathe if you just opened your mouth.

"Congratulations," your lawyer says as she pats you on the back. And you wonder what you did that was right. But instead you say a polite "Thank you," and turn to your now-ex-wife. Each measuring the distance between. Her lawyer, better with a ruler than either of you, wraps your now ex-wife in her arm and guides her out.

DIVORCED—The word follows you down the marble hallway of city hall. Like the Scarlet Letter, a large "D" hangs in the air about you. It's followed you from your middle class roots. *What will the neighbors say? What will grandma think?* The past encircles you like a tree lined cul-de-sac. At home—strange to call the studio apartment "home"—a message from your brother waits for you on the answering machine. He quotes Henry Miller:

I have no money, no resources, no hopes. I am the happiest man alive.

It is time to step inside your television set, to slip through the vertical hold. You are *The Invisible Man, The Creature from the Black Lagoon, The Blob, The Fly*—Yes, Brundle-Fly that is you. Shape changer. Memory Scraper. Change channels and begin again.

LESSON SIX: RENE

The unkempt garden nearly hides the small brick Washington Park bungalow, the path to the front door so overgrown you wonder if anyone lives here at all. Try the doorbell. Nothing. The Lesson is for 5:30. Check your watch. Wait. Is there movement inside? The drawing of the chain, the unbolting of locks. One. Two. Three. *"Hola, Buenas Días,"* the man with a potbelly and long dark hair tied in a ponytail greets you. "Lesson," he says, fixing his gaze somewhere behind you. The door opens to a room with wood floors cleared of all furniture. Posters of dark haired women, their bright red dresses blurred in the rapid-fire heel steps of flamenco, line the walls interspersed with black and white photos of gypsies long since dead. You pass through this room into a smaller one, the walls similarly covered. Two chairs and a music stand make up the only furniture. *"Sientate,"* he says, then disappears for a moment. You sit and tune your guitar.

"Empecemos con una Malagueña," he says, taking the other chair. "Easy."

And you watch the hands of this gypsy from Granada. Big hands.

Knuckled, gnarled hands. Not how you imagine a guitarist's hands to look. You watch this man who grew up performing with his dozen brothers and sisters all over Spain and then the United States. This man who early in his life played on the Ed Sullivan Show. You know this because one of the pictures on the wall shows him with Ed, guitar in hand, the flicker of immortality upon his face. Now his bulbous nose drips with snot, a remnant from the Denver winter. He begins. Plays the opening from Sabicas. "Now you."

You stare back.

"*Venga, coño!*" he curses.

Your fingers stumble through the tremolo—an absurd imitation.

"*No!*" he screams. "*como los gitanos.*" Gypsy style. And his hands demonstrate.

You try again, but can't get it right.

"*No!*"

You can't see the thin skein of ice on the road. Headlights reveal nothing. The 4x4 in front of you spins off to the left. The sedan beside you slides right. "You told me you'd make time for us," your second wife, Tanya, says from the doorway just before you leave for work. "I have," you say. "*Todo mi tiempo es tuya.*" You try to close the door behind you, but she is there. "The writing scares me," she says. "I know you. You won't stop. It's like the fencing. Like the flamenco." You keep walking. Get in the car. Don't look back at the face framed in the doorway of your home.

Hold on while your car spins in circles. Other cars careen around you. A ballet on ice. Nothing left to do but dance.

Before you read John Irving's *The World According to Garp,* before you had any inkling of being a writer, you spent hundreds of hours creating imaginary worlds, wrote thousands of pages detailing the characters in those worlds. Post-Garp, and you realize it was all an escape. What better place to escape in than a dungeon—a labyrinth of your own meticulous construction. Put Demogorgon in the center, and your anarchic world will spin around him. Stay in the center—look out through his eyes dungeon master—and never, ever face the beast. That's it: you control your world. Let the characters in your campaign play out their roles.

You arrive by eight sharp, dressed in slacks, oxford and tie. Your office is bigger than any you have had or ever will have as a teacher. Your window overlooks a park. Very pretty. Just like the pretty picture you paint yourself about finding people work. That's what you do, isn't it. You manage a staffing agency. Find people work. Single mothers. People down on their luck. Others who for reasons all their own want a temp job. And you're happy to oblige. It doesn't hurt that it buys you a house in one of Denver's best neighborhoods. That you can pay for Montessori for your kids. Fly to Spain each summer. Morocco. Buy whatever you wish: Thomasville chairs, Pennsylvania House bedroom set, Kacey Fine Furniture for the living room.

Make your labyrinth so elaborate that no one can penetrate its mysteries. No one can find a way in—or out.

The first two years you devote yourself to business the same way you give yourself to everything else. You eat, sleep, and shit ways to make more money. It's all profit and loss. And like the profits swelling your business, you're beginning to swell. A bit stout about the belly, bloated in the face. The result of sitting all day staring at the computer, talking on the phone. The only exercise you get, the walk across the street to the strip mall restaurants for lunch: *Chipotle, Applebees, Bruegger's Bagels, McDonald's, Subway,* or *Le Peep's*. You're in the business world now. Spend the day thinking of the bottom line. Who needs to be "layed off" because they're not "profitable"? Find them and let them go.

You live in the same house with her. Raise the same two girls. And yet you do not know her. You are sure she knows nothing of you. Was Chekhov right? Is the secret life the truer one or just another of many imagined selves? It's a mystery only those initiated in the suburbs understand. A mystery especially created for those raised to please, to do what is needed to "look good," to "get by." How many false selves can you create so that we all just "get along?"

"It's not enough to read the music," Rene says. "You must have *duende,* feel it."

You concentrate so hard on the finger positions, you feel nothing. But you don't tell him. Instead, you fake your way through a *siguiriya*. He slaps your leg with the back of his hand when you're done. Hard. The next lesson, he simply writes out the notes, nods his head politely when you play them.

You push your wife. Try to take the baby from her. All you can think of is getting out, taking the baby and driving as far away as you can. But when you shove her, you see it as if from the outside. Your hand gripping her arm. The tight lines of her face as she fights to get free. And you want to know who is this person you've become. You tell yourself fencing didn't destroy your first marriage. Flamenco will save your second. You need writing to live, don't you?

You buy a big house in Boulder. A house more expensive than any you dreamed of. And the day after you move in, you wake up and tell your wife: *This is all wrong. We need to get out.* But you don't get out. The hedgerows pull tight about your neck. Keep up the mortgage payment. Keep up with the Jones'. And so eight to five you work. But at night when everyone is asleep, you play your guitar. And on your lunch hour you take lessons. You are always on the verge of reinventing yourself. No more fencing. You abhor the violence of it. The brutality. The ego required to win. (Though if you are honest, not a day goes by in which you don't relive a bout, play out the parry riposte, counter-riposte with your hand.) And no more competition. It's too close to business, too close to laying off old women with cancer, to firing depressives who can't "tow the line." So, screw competition to the sticking place and bring on the music!

Each time you walk into your flamenco teacher's house you suffer vertigo, dizzy with the fact that this interior from the gypsy caves of Granada exists here in one of Denver's oldest neighborhoods—the original suburb. It's as if upon entering you step outside time, back into a past that no longer exists. And you step outside place—to a space light years away from the strip mall anchored by Target and

Marshall's two blocks away. The fact that these interior spaces exist never ceases to amaze you. It's the same with fencing clubs, though they're usually located far from residential neighborhoods—where the real estate is too pricey. Look for them on the other side of the tracks, in the worst parts of town. Search for them in abandoned warehouses and factories, next to porn theaters and Army Surplus stores.

You seek out these inner spaces. But lately that interior space frightens you.

What if when you look within there is nothing but a strip mall?

Your first memory of writing is the dragon research paper for Mrs. Highland's sophomore English class. Sure, you took second prize in the Halloween story contest in third grade, but as far as you remember, you'd simply adapted "Twas the Night Before Christmas." The dragon research paper is something altogether different, you made up all your sources, complete with quotes and in depth citations. You were writing Borges fictions a quarter of a century before you would ever read him. When Mrs. Highland hands back your paper, you're shocked at the large, red "D" and the note to see her after class. You've always gotten A's in English. It's your favorite subject. She asks how you can write a research paper on something that doesn't exist. You tell her what better way to understand a fictional creature than through fictional research. Besides you say, if dragons exist in your imagination, doesn't that make them real? She's not convinced.

To write is to put yourself into the world. To read is to breathe the worlds of others, to take their worlds in as you would take in a lover. Each breath, each ounce of their seed carries with it the worlds of countless others—and so, in your early teens you're ravished by Tolkien, Bradbury, Stephen R. Donaldson, and LeGuin. You nearly die when you read Orwell's *1984*—the little death of the French. Maugham's *Of Human Bondage* licks you awake, and John Irving's *The World According to Garp* gets you hard. Then Faulkner kills you over and over again with *As I Lay Dying, The Sound and the Fury, Absalom, Absalom,* and *Light in August.* You still feel his fetid breath, his body heavy about you, and, like any lover to whom you have lost yourself, you probably always will. Shakespeare, Chaucer and the *Beowulf* poet baptize you in the waters of the word—the potent alchemy of language. Then John Gardner slays you for good, rips bone from sinew as Grendel tears the limbs from the men in Hrothgar's hall. And now, you are eternally trapped in the *breosthord.* Wandering lost in a *swefna cyst* from which you never want to escape.

And so you rise at five in the morning and write. Science fiction stories at first. But they're harder than they look. Then "literary fiction," whatever that is. Stories based on your travels. It's easier to write exotic stories of other worlds than face your own banality.

Flashes of light and dark as you wind your way through the *medina* in Marrakech. Black, goatskin tarps shade the alleys to darkness. Suddenly you cannot see. Bodies push past. Women in *haiks.* Men in flowing *djellabas.* The impossible smell of excrement and pepper. Orange blossoms and urine. The musk of mule. You inhale it deeply and feel the rush of blood, the pounding of your pulse. Slowly, you make your way past doorway after doorway, looking for the exit. Stay close to your wife, your sister-in-law. But then how easy it would be to lose yourself in the crowd, to slip down a winding passage into darkness. What's to stop you from taking on another life? Live somewhere else. Love someone else.

The cry of the *muezzin* calls to you from the tall *minaret. Allaha Ackbar, Allaha Ackbar, Ashhadu al-la ilaha illa Allah.* You gaze out through the wood shutters of your stifling hot hotel room at the edge of the Sahara. The sands of the *Erg Chebbi* float before you, an endless sea. Shut your eyes and sleep.

Hide in the car after the trip to the grocery store. Take extra time in the bathroom. Pretend to go to sleep, then get up and write. Don't let anyone see you. And maybe, just maybe you can squeeze into that dark hole, that space where you feel the slow distillation of time. Hold there while the phone rings, while your wife calls you, while your children jump through the room. Reach your hand out. Can you feel it? That moment that slips through your palm, that brief instant when you are a god?

Suddenly, mornings before work no longer provide enough time to write. You enter the darkness but can't get out, stumbling helplessly down the wrong tunnel. You recall the decomposed bodies of rats in the sewer of your youth. And there is only one way out. So, close your office door, turn the monitor away from the window, forget about finding jobs for others and work on saving yourself.

LESSON SEVEN: BETSY

Setting: The woods at the edge of the world in Bennington, Vermont. Your shirt sticks to your back, the sweat circling under your arms. The droning insects drown everything. At night, they almost do you in, creeping through the broken window screen of your dorm. Your sheets stained with blood in the morning. Even now, as you talk, you can't quite get comfortable. You scratch your ankles, your neck, sure they are coming for you. And yet the woman sitting on the lawn chair before you seems unbothered by any of it, or worse, marks time to the music.

"You've got to let yourself fall in that hole, Peter," she says, her thick Tennessee accent belying the import of her words. "You need to walk through the darkness to find the thing that shines."

At first you don't want to listen. You're a child of science, or at least science fiction. A skeptic by nature, you value only the rational mind. But she sends you totems in the mail. First, a simple rock, then another with a fossil in it. She writes you letters telling you to hold the totem in your hand as you begin your stories. You try it, and your stories change. You don't know if it's the result of the totem, but you're no longer writing Carver or Hemingway rip-offs. And then she begins calling, leaving poetry on your answering machine as your brother had once done.

You do not have to be good.

You do not have to walk on your knees for a hundred miles

through the desert repenting...

To write is to forget the self (or selves), to resurrect the spirit. But how to say what needs to be said when you are a coward?

You do not have to be good.

You skulk through your fiction, slither through poetry.

You do not have to walk on your knees...

Habitualization devours us. It's the old you who filtered your feelings through others, said what others wanted you to say. Right? That's how you've led your life so far. Let yourself be defined by the definitions of others?

Do you solemnly swear to love, honor, and obey the definitions imposed on you by your parents, your family, your spouse?

I do.

Better to hide within the page than to face the self. The only thing more frightening is never to have written at all.

"These stories aren't true," she says the next time you meet in the café in Bennington. "What I mean is, they aren't true to your spirit. I read them, and they sound good, but they dance around the hole. When are you going to let yourself fall in?"

Her blue eyes pierce, and there is nowhere to run.

Lying, as defined by St. Thomas Aquinas, is "a statement at variance with the mind." It is therefore possible to lie without making a false statement or without the intention of deceiving others. Lie, fucker, lie. Write and lie.

LESSON EIGHT: HEDA

"You must have compass," your second flamenco teacher says, and by that he means you have to feel the rhythm. You're both crammed into a small practice booth above the music store. There are no pictures. Only the cream colored walls that remind you of the womb, you mean your home. He turns his guitar over and pats out the rhythm on the back. "Now you." These two phrases are the only ones he seems to know in English. You want to respond in Spanish since it's your only foreign language, but that's no good either. He speaks Farsi. Rhythm is the only form of communication left to you. He pounds out the rhythm again. And again, you hesitate. What's blocking your synapses? You can hear it. Why is the signal not going from your ears to your hands? What is it the brain cannot translate? You concentrate so hard it hurts. It won't come.

And yet, though you don't understand each other, though you barely understand the music, something of its rhythm seeps into you so that by the end of the hour you have a language—a dream language that starts to fade the moment you leave the eight by eight practice booth. Desperate, you run to your car in the downtown parking lot. Take your guitar out of its case, sit on the bumper —yes, cling to the last pulse, grasp the last fleeting remnant before it fades.

Writing is another form of rhythm. As Flaubert said, "The human tongue is like a cracked cauldron on which we beat out tunes to set a bear dancing when we would make the stars weep with our melodies." You write to beat your self into the world. Like some magician of the black arts, some succubus conjured from a dark and ancient world, you want to send your spirit into the body of another, to possess that other completely, to force them to feel the contours of your being, the shape of your very soul. Is it purely a masculine yearning? It is certainly sexual. A joining with another. And if writing is masculine, does that make reading the feminine? We read to let the other in. The search always for the book that will ravish you, take you over completely. There's a reason those books are few and far between. Great lovers are rare. And so, we are all hermaphrodites, each searching desperately for the half we already contain.

He is so different from your first guitar teacher. Slender. Long wiry hair. Fine features. His manner is different, too. Softer. And though he never seems to grow impatient with your bumbling attempts to imitate his playing, he pushes you hard, much harder than the gypsy from Granada, who in the end gave up on you, never asking you to play anything more than the notes. Never again mentioning rhythm. Style. Passion. What it means to play music another human being will hear. Heda forces you to play—over and over. He'll only repeat the phrase twice—three times if it's particularly hard. Then he will not play it again. He will set his guitar down, cross his arms, bring one hand up to his face and rest his chin in the crook between the thumb and forefinger. He'll sit and wait with the patience of a sadistic lover.

"Can you play it one more time?" you beg.

He doesn't answer.

All you ask for is a flash of awareness. A moment. But the television static sounds in your head. And you can't adjust your set because you can't find the remote.

If you can do it in writing, you can do it in music. And so, you push through the fact that the country you come from knows nothing of the rhythms of flamenco—its twelve beat rhythms so different from blues, rock or jazz. You push through your own DNA's resistance to playing on the off beat. You push through your own limited musical ability—though you've played guitar most of your life, you've never progressed beyond bar chords for the most basic of rock anthems. And you push through your fear that all this is for naught, that you're fooling yourself to think you can ever play something so complicated, something made only for people who grew up on the syncopated crack of guitars, the *rasqueados* that scrape the back of their necks as they sit at the guitarist's feet. You push through every bit of resistance, force your hands to beat out the rhythm, falteringly at first, the second try not much better, working to scratch the beat in your memory. No. Deeper. Dig that well deep. Pray to strike a pool, some ancient memory of rhythm. And, as always, you sweat. The air conditioning in the practice room could be running full. Hell, it could be snowing and you'd still sweat.

Can you explain this need to your wife? To your friends, your family? How explain the need to make art of your life when no language exists? It's in the white space, within the caesuras, beyond the end-stops, in the space between words. Places that can only be intuited—and then, even then, you must be willing to sit and wait for meaning to come. Only stillness keeps the static at bay.

You're after immortality, but not the kind that comes in books. Not the kind packaged and sold at a fifteen percent discount in Wal Mart. Eternity is found in a well-honed sentence, a perfectly executed *rasqueado,* or *finta in tempo.* It's gone the second you realize it's there. If you look, it's too late. Leave that to the critics and posers. Meanwhile crawl into your hole, stare down the darkness. If it blinds you, so much the better.

When you're done, Heda says the only other English phrase he knows: "It's good, but you must practice." It doesn't matter. You go on hoping that maybe you can step out of your white bread, middle class, suburban life and set your foot in the world of the *roma,* the gypsy.

Before you pack up your guitar, you share a glance, and you know he lives in the space between words. It nearly kills you. After, you carry your guitar down the residential streets lined with pre-fab houses, past trees planted—one in each yard—to give the neighborhood an older feel, and you believe you carry something older still.

LESSON NINE: RIKKI

From outside, the house looks like any other. Open the door and your nose is overwhelmed: orange blossom, sandalwood, and myrrh. She greets you in long, flowing robes. A kiss on the cheek, then she escorts you inside. The graduate students sit around a dark, Quaker table near the kitchen. Several pots of tea boil on the stove. At least four or five cakes add cranberry, lemon, and cinnamon to the concatenation of smells.

She serves you, waits until you're full. You remember the story of "Hansel and Gretel" and are on your guard as she sits at the head of the table. She sifts through the pile of manuscripts, her face betraying nothing, then makes her pronouncements:

"This is crap." She takes the top manuscript from the pile and throws it on the floor. "We're not going to waste our time on it."

She takes the next manuscript, peels back the first page. "This is crap." And it, too, falls to the floor.

Again, "This is crap."

She comes to your manuscript. Looks over the first page, peers at the second, moves as if to toss it aside, then stops. "This is so bad, it's almost not worth discussing."

She then spends the next hour talking about how awful your piece was.

"Yet, there is something," she says.

You listen between her words, search for a hint of what she means.

"Sliver of imagination…"

There it is. You heard it, or think you did. You try to catch more but come away with nothing.

Nothing, except the fact that there was something.

Your next piece is better. She's actually curious about it, wondering at your use of the Billy Goat as an alter ego for your protagonist's desires. She speaks of the alchemy of language, the need to move beyond the simple definitions of things, to bring the dream to life.

That you understand. You live a waking dream, never sure exactly where or who you are.

You make an excuse to go to the bathroom, but really you need time to be alone, to feel your way through the forest. Down the stairs and to the left. You pass a dark room, the door slightly ajar. You can't help but peer inside. Her artwork covers the walls, a half finished piece still on the easel: a yellow fruit, split open upon a red background. The paint is still wet. You breathe it in. The damp wood smell. Turpentine. Take it all in so that you won't forget, can't forget. Stay as long as you dare.

You create your own space in the basement, line it with books, shut the door and lock it. Here there be Monsters. It works! Your children are afraid to come down, sure they'll be gobbled up.

You cover the walls with art, play music at full volume, recite poetry to yourself—anything to push out the external world, to give you a chance to fall into the hole. And there you discover your own deep banality.

Language is quicksilver. Words can change shape. You must

believe this. And so you search for the philosopher's stone, for the imaginative power to transform your own inner suburbia. And every once in a while you find it. You see your world with hyper-clarity, its colors distorted, or perhaps reflecting a truer hue. You are the artist, and as Klee says, the world rises through you, transformed.

But who are you fooling? Those moments don't make up a life. Add them all up even for the greatest guitarists, the Olympic medalists, and Nobel laureates, and you might account for a few minutes. A few grains of sand in a vast hourglass. The rest is a fight. And this fight is with yourself. So how do you win? Stab the fucker! Kill the TV self and another will rise to take its place. Strangle the child of strip malls and watch another walk back through the electronic, sliding glass doors and into the cool comfort of air conditioning, Slurpee in hand.

The where are you now category: You know the talk. Where's that B level rocker past his prime who has slipped into obscurity. Old actors are easy to spot when they've lost their edge. You used to see them on *Hollywood Squares*. Now it's *Dancing with the Stars!* But rockers are a different breed. When their hair starts receding and their paunches start growing, they rarely go gently. Instead, they reassemble for one last "Reunion Tour," a tour that goes on and on, year after never-ending year, making millions. So what about old fencers? Flamenco wannabes? Academic writers?

Three kids. No dog. Twenty-two hundred square foot house on a five thousand two hundred and twenty-six square foot plot with two trees in the front yard and two in back. (You know the measurements of your world well.) Second house from the end of the cul-de-sac. Wave to the neighbors as you drive by. Take out the trash every Sunday night. Be sure to get the recyclables in their proper containers.

Often, your first thought on weekends is to head to the mall with your own kids. You resist it, but sometimes you don't. They have everything there: play areas, cookie shops, ice cream, air conditioning and merry-go-rounds—even jumpy castles. Clothing stores for kids and clothes for you. Housewares. Jewelry. Sunglasses. Cell Phones. Even Hermit Crabs. You bought two—named them Hermit and Sebastian (Guess why?). It seems easier than going on a hike, where you have to spread sunscreen on the kids' faces, make sure they wear a hat, wash the dust from their clothes after and be ready to carry them when they say they can't walk anymore. In a mall, you can sit in the air conditioning and eat ice cream. You can rest your weary legs on plastic benches, looking out over the vast expanse of the food court, wondering what you'll eat next.

Sometimes you take the kids camping in the minivan. Lot number six set along the river and right between two RV's. Get your bundle of wood so you can cook S'mores over your designated "fire pit." Lie awake at night freezing in your tent, wondering when this particular package of nature will deliver its promise, when you can climb into the burnt hull of that redwood and fall back into the breath of creation. I'm sorry. No noise between 10 p.m and 8 a.m. And you must leave your site by noon. Thanks, the management.

You take a night out without the kids. A night amongst friends to remedy your chronic emptiness. But when you arrive, you see your body sitting in the chair talking about how the *tapas* aren't bad for the States, how it would be better to get there at eight-thirty and avoid the crowds, how the latest Bruce Willis movie really did have something to say, how the woman at the table next to yours is just so fat, and you know that you must behave. Fake it. Say the words, but leave yourself at home. It's only polite. Consciousness can be dangerous. Better to drift away to searing hot nights in Andalucia.

DAY ONE: ARCOS DE LA FRONTERA

Climb dark alleyways dodging speeding Vespas. Navigate cobblestone paths laid out in labyrinthine patterns. A man steps through a doorway you would swear wasn't there a minute ago. "Flamenco?" he asks. "Sí," you reply, and he opens the door. You climb a stairway that spills out into the ruins of a cathedral atop a cliff. The entire town is gathered, sitting in chairs, on crumbled walls, standing amongst the rubble. A stage with two chairs is set in the ruins of the nave. An old man dressed in a thin button up shirt and dark slacks and a teenage boy dressed all in black carrying a guitar mount the stage. You are the only foreigner, and as the music falls, you weep.

DAY TWO: JEREZ

One hour in the guitar store *Valeriano Bernal* and rarely have you felt so alive. Alfonso says guitars are like people, each one has a unique soul. The guitarist must sound the wood, searching for his soulmate. You take the first guitar in your hands, a sunburst one made of cypress and spruce. And though you have much to talk about, the conversation remains at the level of the weather. You wandered so long in the one hundred and ten degree heat, lost in the streets searching for the store, that by the time you arrived you were drenched. The sweat seeping through your armpits, across your back and chest. You wipe the beads from your brow before they drip onto the next guitar, a blonde of cypress and cedar. As you strike the strings, you think this might be it. But Alfonso tells you to wait. He sees in you a sadness that calls for something different. He tells you to be patient while he restrings a guitar made of dark wood—*la negra,* he calls it. And so you wait, hoping to cool down, to stop sweating, though there is no air conditioning in the store. He hands you the guitar, and you strike up a *siguiriya,* a *cante hondo,* the saddest of songs. This is the one, you tell Alfonso. Though you don't buy it. The money is already spent for your daughter's piano lessons. Someday, you tell yourself. Someday.

Each city also has its soul. The soul of Jerez is an old man sitting on a park bench, his pants held up by a rope. You sit beside him, and he tells you of the death of his wife eleven years ago. He talks of his three daughters, two still near, one in Madrid. He speaks proudly of his four grandchildren, how the three-year-old looks just like the soccer star, Beckham. And with a sigh, he recounts how his kidneys are failing, how he started dialysis a month ago, and how he is approaching *"kilometro cuatro."*

"Do you know what that means?" he asks.

"No," you say.

"The cemetery lies four kilometers outside the city," he says with a grim laugh.

You offer him some of your ham, your Manchego cheese, and you talk of the barbarity of the death penalty in the States. The Iraq war. He tells you he doesn't understand, and you say you don't either.

When he goes, he leaves you his newspaper.

"Hasta luego," you say, though you know you'll never see him again.

"Hasta otra," he replies, and you wonder if perhaps he understands more than you. "Until another time." It's a good phrase, you think. Another time. Who knows when or where that might be? Tomorrow. A year from now. After death. When the world ends or before the beginning of the next?

This is no mid-life crisis. You won't find anything so clichéd as a red corvette, a black Audi Turbo TT, or a yellow convertible in your driveway. No earrings, pony tails, or tattoos please. No young blonde hanging on your arm. No back to the "good 'ol days," bowling with the boys—the days before responsibility. This is nothing. *Nada*. There's no escape. No Quarter. And you won't ask for any.

So, before you continue. Take a moment to look out from the obscurity of middle-age. Tell me what you see. Who is your opponent standing on the opposite end of the strip, blade in hand, mask tucked under his arm?

You see the world of Prozac and crystals, aromatherapy and reiki, Deepak Chopra and Dr. Phil, jogger strollers and Baby Bjorns, massage therapists and Feng shui, cigars and sushi, single malt scotch and tequila, vacations in Maui, vacations in Cancun, Vegas. *Did you hear about our trip to Puerto Rico? The beaches are fantastic. The hotel superb. We never left the beach.* Date nights: Dinner and a movie. Movies. Movies. Movies. Internet. Gameboy. MTV. "Reality TV." Any TV. Jogging. Biking. Hiking. Triathalon. Xtreme Sports. Have to get your workout in. Need a break from the job. A break from the kids. A break from life. A break. Everything is a break.

At night, you dream of Jerez. Of Cordoba. Granada. But these are mere physical places. Though they open the doorway to the world you seek, to rely on them is need, a crutch, a fix. To think otherwise is to delude yourself. To follow the same false prophet as the "entertained," the "physically fit," the "thrill seekers," alcoholics and drug addicts. As Rumi says, "I have stood on the lip of insanity, knocking on the door. It opens. I've been knocking from the wrong side."

The god you seek lies within. It's your most intimate truth.

Look through the door and what do you see?

The times when your deep suburban life takes on a different hue. You see the sepia tones that slip in with the sunset as you ride your bike with your children in circles round and round the cul-de-sac. You see them in the symmetry of the lines as you sit on the park bench with your wife, sipping wine and chatting to the neighbors as your kids run through the freshly mown grass. And you see them in the entire palate of colors that paint your son's face when he first takes his tricycle down the driveway. Just look through the door, damn you! It's all there, kissing your life as sweetly as any finely honed sentence. *Touché!* Point to your opponent. *En-garde, s'il vous plait.* Wait! I can't see it. *Êtes vous prêt?* No! It's too dark in this mask. Give me a moment. I need to wipe the sweat from my eyes.

"Flamenco is very simple," Heda says as you're leaving the practice studio. "There are only two things you have to remember. To listen and to watch."

It's too simple, you want to say. But then you know, it is the most difficult thing of all.

Listen and Watch. Yes, Heda.

POSTSCRIPT #1

The old man (who is you, at least you think it's you, at least in the dream it feels like you) arrives first. He walks through the dark hall, the sound of each footstep on the wood floor echoing through his mind, awakening him slowly from his stupor. He paces the circumference of the room, reacquainting himself with his world, measuring its limits. He is not aware of what is happening inside him during this time, or if he is, it is an awareness only felt in the body, so that when he moves to unlock the iron bars covering the great windows, when he opens them, allowing the outside air to flow in, it's not because he has decided the hall is stuffy. It is simply time to breathe. One at a time, he switches on the chandeliers, though there is a master he could use. Like the old man, the building needs time to wake from its languor, to step out of the past, or, rather, out of the present. After all, it's only through the sound of steel ringing through the old hall that the building gains its voice.

The building was constructed as a German dance hall in 1886, yellow and brown brick on the outside, a polished wood floor reflecting the light from two-dozen chandeliers on the inside. Nobody dances there anymore, which is fitting. The building is an anachronism, nestled between a porn theater and a Burger King. It sits, patiently, waiting for the coming of night and the fencers with their white knickers and iron masks, their bags filled with swords.

The old man (Peter is his name. You are sure of it now—though in the end the name doesn't matter) is by far the oldest of the fencers present. And, he is the first one dressed in his knickers and jacket. The first to don his glove and mask. He must then endure the waiting once again, as he watches the younger men and women chat about work, family, the weather. They don't come for the same reason he does; he knows that. They don't need it as he does; or, if they do, it is only felt as one feels hunger in a dream: dimly, approximately.

The history of the sword is the history of man. He understands this. Though it is only in small part because of the violence, the blood spilt. The fight has more to do with the need to match one's inner rhythm to another, a need closer to procreation than death, a desire to conjoin rather than destroy.

With a nod of his head, he signals a younger man in his forties to join him on the strip. The man smiles, though he looks pained that he must now don his mask and make the effort. The younger man's hair is receding; his eyes shot with red. He drags the point of his blade on the ground as he walks to the strip. He manages one of the temporary staffing agencies in the city. (Is he not also you? One of infinite versions spun into the world with each decision, each fork in the road. You hope not but fear otherwise.)

The old man waits. Rarely does he make the first move, preferring to study his opponent. *Is his guard high or low? Does he keep his hand too far to the inside? How does he prepare his attack? Does he charge without thought? Are his first steps tentative and small?* The man with the receding hairline (Why does the hair recede on this younger version and not the older? Where is the logic in that?) advances, but he waits too long to attack, he has fenced the old man before and is wary of the man's lightening-quick hand. The old man lunges forward on legs that should have given out long ago, but that somehow, only when he is fencing, respond as they did thirty years before.

The old man only stopped fencing once in his life, for six months following a horse riding accident when he was forty-nine. (This part of the dream never makes sense because you don't particularly like horses, they frighten you—though you have always imagined owning a ranch in the mountains, living the life of a cowboy. Who doesn't?) High in the Colorado Rockies, something spooked the horse; he imagined it had been a mountain lion, watching from the rocks above, studying him the same way he'd studied countless opponents. He never knew for sure. The horse reared, knocking him off; then, losing its own balance, the horse fell on him, crushing his femur. The man was lucky he ever walked again. Sitting in the hospital bed, he fought battle upon battle in his mind, imagining different opponents and various scenarios. *You are fencing the Russian who loves to counter-attack, and you are losing the bout. Push him to the edge, then make second intention to play off his habit!* The only sign that his mind was working at all as he laid in the hospital bed was the telltale movement of his hand as it acted out the parries and thrusts.

His opponent, the younger man with the receding hairline, fences as if it were a chore, throwing his body forward to attack. He doesn't understand that a properly executed lunge is different than closing a deal. (It is at this point that you almost wake up. It is too much, you say. How can each version of you be so different?)

The old man sets the rhythm, slow, a waltz by Strauss. He must conserve his speed, store it for when it is needed. The younger man is happy to oblige the slower pace. Lulled into relaxation, he welcomes the respite to catch his breath. The old man strikes in between the beats of the Waltz, his speed now that of an up-tempo swing. Having lost the touch, the younger man's shoulders slouch; he jams the point of his blade into the floor; he lopes back down the strip.

The old man senses something stirring in his opponent. He hopes it is desire, but knows it is more likely anger. He signals with his hand for the next encounter to begin. His opponent charges, his foil spinning like a windmill. The old man retreats, then, suddenly, thrusts his point high—too high to score a valid touch, but high enough that his opponent sees it. The younger man stops, flailing for his opponent's blade. Finding it, he attacks. The old man is ready, having determined this moment. He hammers home a quick parry four riposte to the chest. Now is the most dangerous time in the bout. The old man repeats this to himself. He never lets himself forget. He has seen many a man relax when he has gained the advantage. He himself has done the same; it is the most natural thing of all—to stop working, to think it can come easy.

Again, he signals for the action to begin. The younger man doesn't move. He wants the old man to come to him. He wants to take advantage of the old man's slower legs. He wants it to be easy. The younger man makes a half step forward, his sword arm too low. *He's drawing me in*, the old man thinks. And then he advances, obliging, lunges short, as he is expected to do. His opponent blocks his attack and sends his own directly to the collarbone of the old man's sword arm. Though the old man is prepared for the attack, he is not prepared for the precision of its placement. *He is capable of surprises*, the old man thinks. *He noticed the six parry is my weakness.*

The score is tied at four a piece. The next touch wins. *He is learning,* the old man thinks, and he smiles. *He's been studying me.* The old man doesn't curse himself for letting down his guard. There is no time for that. His younger opponent is upon him, throwing everything he has into this one last assault. At first, he attempts to run the old man down. But the old man slows his opponent with false cuts and jabs. Frustrated, the younger man lunges a half-step too soon. He wants so badly to finish it. Overextending himself in a hopeless attempt to reach the old man, he exposes his back. Like a matador, the old man steps forward, his blade high in the air, the point aimed downward. He drives it into the younger man's back.

They salute. The old man gazes into his rival's eyes as they shake hands. And for a moment, before the younger man looks away, there is acknowledgement. The old man knows the young man's desperation. He has felt it before. The young man understands the old man's need, if only ephemerally. Like Sancho at his master's deathbed, the younger man understands too late that only by returning to the fight is there any hope.

The old man walks off the strip to wait his turn for another match. He stands in the corner by the great, iron-framed window, while the others huddle around the water cooler. He breathes deeply as the night air enshrouds him. In these moments, in between bouts, he doesn't think of what will happen if he ever stops, if he misses even one night. Those thoughts come in the morning, when he first awakens and feels the fluid draining from the disks of his spine, evaporating from his joints, replaced by hard minerals that stiffen and irritate. He rubs his shoulders and arms, reshaping the porous, moth eaten bone. He studies his finger joints as if he can see their thickening, then takes each finger of his right hand and kneads it.

The fencers gather together to head to the corner pub. Before they leave, the younger man breaks from the crowd. He asks the old man if he would like to join them, though the old man has never done so before. But the old man says he would prefer to clean up. If the younger man had stayed to watch, perhaps he would have understood.

The old man's world is fourteen meters long by two meters wide. A bigger kingdom than most, and he does not wish for more. He paces it. Every night for the last fifty-four years he's staked it out—sometimes with tape, other times with shoes, plastic cups. Anything will do. And, afterwards, he cleans it up. Leaves no trace. To leave a shred of tape on the hard wood floor would be like waking prematurely, breaking the dream into fragments. And he could not bear that. Only by disassembling his world, piece by piece, then placing it all in the storage locker in the basement of the building, can he keep it whole—at least until the next night.

He has done it this way every night since he saw the ad in the college paper as a freshman. Only when he smells the thick odor of sweat from his jacket, inhales the fetid air trapped in the iron mesh of his mask does he move toward consciousness; only when he hears the clang of steel, when he wraps his hand around the grip, the way one might hold a bird, does he really breathe. The day leading up to this moment is a long sleep; the night after is haunted by memories of what it means to live. If he stops, he will die. The old man knows this. It is his daily deliberate choice that keeps him fighting, helps him to endure the sleep of the present only to awaken each night in the past.

And so you wake, only to fall into another dream.

POSTSCRIPT #2

Wait for dusk's fading light. *Espera.* When the voice of the *cantaor* summons the gathering shadows, peer out from your hotel room. Listen for the crack of the *tocaor's* fingers upon the guitar strings. Fall into the space between the beats of the *palmas.* Let slip time, place. Direction no longer matters here. North. South. East. West. None have meaning. Only rhythm exists. Without it you are lost in the labyrinth. *Entonces,* follow the flickering shadows as they climb the ancient stone walls of Calle Céspedes, drift among them toward mecca as you merge onto Calle Blanco Belmonte, follow it back to the homeland of the moors on Alta de Santa Ana straight until you run into the Plaza Jerónimo Páez, and there at last you will find me—a shadow on the hot Cordoban stones.

Wait.

The heat rises, and I am released.

How did we get here? It's as if the other life was a dream. And this life is all that matters. This life in the trash-strewn plaza, graffiti marking the walls. The rancid smell of piss and human sweat. Shit-stained stones. Breathe deeply of it.

A lone white plastic table caked with coffee and jam stains, breadcrumbs, a shred or two of *jamon serrano*, leftovers from careless tourists. Cigarette butts spill out of the lone ashtray in the center. No one wipes off this table. Not ever. A glass stands empty upon it, coffee dregs within. Two men sit there, both with long black hair falling about their shoulders. Gray streaks the shorter man's hair. Gray also in the scruff that dirties his face. He sits with feet flat on the stone, fingers interlaced in his lap, head bowed, waiting. The taller sits with legs crossed, his guitar poised against him. Hands like wings, hands that could take flight at any moment, hold the guitar in the cradle of his legs. Note how he begins. Study how he takes the neck carefully in his left hand, his thumb set firmly into the nape, his fingers wrapping about the neck as if it were a woman he was about to take for his pleasure. He takes his time with his opening *rasqueado*, each finger stroking the strings, one after another. Slowly, he slides into a tremolo. The shorter man lifts his head. His glasses are too big for his face. He turns his hands palms up before him, in supplication. His gut protrudes through a broken button in the bottom of his shirt, his pants held up by rope. He would seem comical except for the howl of pain that rips from his throat.

Soy grande por ser Gitano…

The guitarist hits the body of his guitar, marking the twelve beat count. (It's you as you've always wanted to look. Long silken hair. Jet black. A week's stubble upon your cheek. Chin chiseled like a poem.) Crack. He strikes the offbeat as if only there the singer will find his voice.

White light of the moon cast upon once-fired stones. Winds rustling through olive and sycamore leaves.

She steps from the darkness, hands, snakelike, writhe above her head. Face set in profile as if a clear view of the full lips, the high cheekbones, the burning angle of the eyes would overhwelm any man. Hips undulate to the slowly building rhythm, each footstep in answer to the repeated pulsing of the guitar.

The singer calls to her

She shakes her head in response.

He calls again.

She flicks her red skirt in his direction. In response to her mood, the slap of her hands upon her thighs, the guitarist ups the tempo with a crack upon the strings. The rhythm he sets acting like ether, like some medium that connects the other two, singer and dancer. And so, as he beats out the tempo, he also determines the pulse of their desire.

The singer raises his hand before him like some medieval magician conjuring spirits, and he lets loose a cry at once of despair and exultation.

The dancer steps before him, takes the rhythm deep, until her back arches, her arms fall to her sides.

And then, the beating cypress breath of the guitar. Her breasts rise and fall with each respiration. The backs of her hands move to her eyes. A veil which she slowly lifts.

The singer's cry builds in strength as the guitarist's tempo increases, then shatters into phrases that mean nothing in and of themselves but that ride the breaking cadence of the guitarist's rhythm.

The dark-eyed dancer answers in kind, taking her skirt in hand, first wrapping it about her then slowly peeling it away. She marks time, slapping hands, hips, thighs, gazing only at the singer.

Hands of the guitarist flash in the moonlight. Incorporeal. Like a god flayed upon an ancient altar, he trembles as he strikes the final strum on his guitar. The sound hangs in the air.

He lays his guitar face down upon his lap. Signals to the waiter for another coffee and waits. He thinks of the deep cut lines about the singer's eyes and brow. The thick glasses and paunch.

And he hopes that when he is that age, he will be able to look in the mirror and whisper to himself: *Go to hell.*

(It's then you look down at your hands. They are yours, aren't they? The same bulge in the first knuckle of the pinky on your left hand where you broke it playing basketball as a kid, the same middle two fingers of your right hand that lean into each other because of the spiral fracture you got fencing for the gold. You look but you're no longer sure. Suddenly, you want to know whether you're the guitarist. You want to know more than anything. Maybe you really are the singer. Maybe your time has been well spent, and you are approaching *kilometro cuatro.*)

As if to be sure, the guitarist downs the last dregs of his coffee, takes up his guitar once again to practice his *arpeggios, tremolos,* and *rasqueados,* to play until his fingers won't work anymore.

The sun drifts like smoke over the horizon, winding its way through cobblestone streets. The bell of a cathedral rings throughout the plaza. The guitarist stops to listen.

A cell phone blares behind him, and his world zooms into focus. The recording of the cathedral bell catches, repeating itself over and over again. The sun's glare reveals the freshly painted plaster of a fake plaza ala Disneyland. Across from him, the bright yellow McDonald's sign shines garishly upon the carefully constructed remains of a replica of a roman wall. Starbuck's opens its doors fashioned to resemble the gateway to the *plaza do toros* in Ronda, and the aroma of a thousand venti lattes floods over the linoleum patterned with *azulejos*. Plastic palms sway in the breeze around the perimeter.

The guitarist rises, packs his guitar in its case and wanders back the way he came, but everywhere he turns is another storefront, another facade. He searches out the alleys, cuts his way through piles of old newspaper and empty wine bottles, careful to step over the dog shit, and hides behind a dumpster, waiting again for night to fall. And as the sun beats down upon him, he wonders which is the dream.

He tells himself to wake up.

The afternoon sears his flesh. By three he can scarcely remember the fragrant scent of the Lady of the Night drifting down upon the breeze. A few minutes more, and the cool breath of jasmine has receded. His legs go to sleep and he shifts positions, doomed to this life beneath the sun.

Four o'clock. He turns his mind within. Waiting there for the setting of the sun. It begins with smoke rising from his fingertips, his scalp, his feet. Then a slow burning sensation over his skin. His hands are the first to catch fire, the flame arcing from finger to finger, then sparking to his chest, burning the hair there, then skin, heart, blood and bone. Immolation. Cinders to ash.

At last the sun sets. And the first breeze of evening winds its way through the streets and back alleys, picking up papers and ash, swirling him up until he climbs the high stone and is released into the night.

POSTSCRIPT #3

You're reading it. Dreamed almost exactly as you wished it to be.

Wake again only to fall into yet another dream. Or dream and fall into another period of waking. It is your choice. Have it however you prefer.

ACKNOWLEDGEMENTS

"All or Nothing at the Fabergé" appeared (minus the footnotes) in *Post Road #11* and was also short listed for a Pushcart Prize in 2007.